Also Plays

Stories from a Middlebury Life

by Karl Lindholm
Dean of Advising Emeritus, Middlebury College

Introduction by David Stameshkin
Middlebury College Historian

ONION
RIVER
PRESS

191 Bank Street
Burlington, Vermont 05401

Printed in the United States of America
ISBN 9781949066005

Onion River Press
191 Bank Street
Burlington VT 05401

For Erica and Frank

Introduction

I first came upon the writing of Karl Lindholm back around 1988 when—deeply entrenched in researching the second volume of my magisterial history of Middlebury College (now sold in drug stores in the sleep-aid section)—I was leafing through back issues of the *Middlebury Magazine*. Karl had written, for the Spring 1986 edition, a short, bittersweet recollection of the 1966–67 Middlebury men's varsity basketball team, of which he was a member and occasional starter, that managed to earn only one victory in its 25 games. It was very well written, and one line in particular grabbed me. "Players on that team were largely one-dimensional athletes, but they were multi-dimensional individuals," he wrote. "The team, and the intensity of our commitment to one another and the ever so elusive success of victory, was the alembic of our friendship." I remember saying to myself how I fervently hoped this guy would keep writing.

Some prayers ARE answered!

Karl, perhaps in preparation for his 50th Middlebury College reunion in the spring of 2017, has put together more than 100 short vignettes that provide, among other things, one man's take on some of the important changes and continuities at the College in the past half-century. These stories are, indeed, "a view from the ground," as he describes and characterizes many of the Middlebury "trees" and yet never loses his understanding of the forest. And he doesn't flinch from relating the bad times as well as the good in both his own life at Middlebury and the College's life during his four years as an undergraduate and past four decades as a dean and faculty member.

Karl's stories range from loving—even sentimental—portraits of former classmates and colleagues to very funny experiences and very sad ones, as well. I had trouble putting this book down, and I believe you will, too.

In the spring of 1974, as I began my research on the first volume of my history of the College, I was conducting a group discussion with members of the Class of 1924 at their 50th Reunion. Reginald "Doc" Cook '24, the legendary Middlebury professor of American Literature, was there with his classmates. At some point, I asked them what they did at night after dinner in their undergraduate years. Doc quickly offered that the curriculum was difficult, "so we just headed for our rooms and four or five hours of studying." The room was silent for about five seconds, before his classmates, one by one, began to laugh—they laughed so hard, they couldn't stop. Finally, one of them managed to gasp, "Doc, YOU were in your room studying! The rest of us were headed downtown or to other places!" Doc turned red, and said, "I never knew."

Fortunately for us, Karl Lindholm—as a student and a dean and now as a retiree— has never been one to head to his room for the night. A fraternity member and varsity jock on both the baseball and basketball teams, Karl was plenty bright, but could not really claim the first half of the scholar-athlete tag until after graduation, when he taught high school English, discovered American Literature, and attended graduate school in American Studies. After that, he became increasingly excited and proficient at both writing and research. His excellent historical publications in recent years on aspects of the era of segregated baseball are infused with his passion for the subject, and demonstrate that his years of teaching writing classes have paid off for him as well as his students.

Full Disclosure: I suppose one of the reasons I love this book so much is that I have a lot in common with Karl. We were both born in 1945, spent an inordinate amount of time working around golf courses in our youth, attended excellent colleges, and earned our PhDs well after receiving our undergraduate degrees. We both taught high school before landing administrative jobs at superb small liberal arts colleges (his somewhat more superb than mine—Franklin & Marshall). We both had some opportunities to teach and do research, and, although we both had the same ultimate career goal of being a Dean of Students, we have always wanted (somewhat desperately) for our faculty colleagues to be cognizant of our abilities as teachers and scholars. We both have taught and done research in areas of African-American history, and we are fanatic sports fans who grew up on Chip Hilton sports books. We share the never-to-be-forgotten experience of being the deans who worked directly with fraternities and alcohol education for many years. We are both married to brilliant and beautiful female academics, who have blessed us with amazing children. Both of us have a special love for Middlebury College. And both of us have now published a memoir of stories—his centered on his life at Middlebury, and mine (*The F**ket List: Things I Will NOT Be Doing Before I Die*) more centered on the first half of my life.

But, I promise, that you don't need to have shared any or all of these experiences to enjoy this book (such as having various liquids tossed at you at fraternity parties that you had been ordered to close down). I swear my liquid was worse than his!

Enjoy!

David Stameshkin
20 March 2017

Also Plays

I told the fabulous Middlebury's men's basketball team in 2010–11 that another Middlebury hoop team had also gone 24–1: the one I played on at Middlebury my senior year. This confused them, as they were sure no team had ever duplicated their success. Then I explained, "We *lost* 24 games and won one."

The symmetry thrills me. It's a palindrome: 24–1 1–24. We're forever connected.

In my junior year we were sent a scouting report of our team from Trinity College, purloined by the brother of a Middlebury friend. Next to the names of our guys was a notation about skills and tendencies: "good shooter, always goes right," that kind of thing.

Next to my name was simply: "Also plays."

An apt description of my career at Middlebury.

Admissible!

Middlebury Dean of Admissions Fred Neuberger was a friend of my dad. They were in the same business. My dad was the Dean of Admissions at Bates College. That's why I didn't go to Bates like everyone else in my family: I couldn't get in.

My dad thought I needed to get out of Lewiston. My sister, a junior at Bates, said, "Go to Middlebury. It's a lot like Bates, only prettier."

The office in Old Chapel in which Fred Neuberger interviewed me for admission to Middlebury in 1963 became mine when I came to work at the College 13 years later.

He asked me two questions, *he* answered them both, and then called in my dad.

"Milt, he's admissible!" Fred exulted.

He was so pleased he didn't have to turn down Milt Lindholm's boy.

Fred

Taking One for the Team

Before choosing Middlebury, I came to visit on a spring weekend.
Fred set it up. I believe he wildly embellished my potential as a
college athlete. I was put up at the DU fraternity, a so-called
"jock house," and treated grandly.

The DU boys fixed me up on a date on Saturday with a wonderful
girl (they were girls then, not women; we were boys), a sophomore named Sue Githens.

Dick Rapp accompanied me to pick up our dates in Forest Hall.
His girlfriend had a memorable name: Melrose Huff.

In the lobby of Forest East, Dick announced himself to the girl
working behind the counter, who dutifully paged his date on the
hall P.A. system: "Melrose Huff, Dick Rapp is here for you."
That was the way it worked then.

Then Dick said to her, "And tell Sue Githens that Gordie Eaton is
here for her," which she did. High-pitched howls emanated from
the hallway: "Gordie Eaton, GORDIE EATON!" they screamed.

Gordie Eaton was a dashing Olympic skier, a Middlebury student.
I was a far cry from Gordie Eaton.

Sue Githens and I went to a party at the DKE House. I was in way
over my head. I was tongue-tied. I didn't dance. I had never even
had a beer so I certainly wasn't drinking. We stood awkwardly for
an hour or so, and then I walked back with her to her dorm.

She took one for the team that night.

Class Dismissed

Passing a lab science was a prerequisite to graduation at Middlebury in the 1960s. I'm not good at math—or science. I took Geology in my first year, "Rocks for Jocks."

Chemistry and physics were out of the question. Biology teachers bragged about how many students flunked the beginning course.

Brewster Baldwin was our geology teacher. What a wonderful man he was. He died just a few months after he retired, alas. He made no concessions to our inaptitude, our ineptitude. He taught the course with seriousness of purpose, a high level of sincerity. I had nothing but respect for him. I liked the labs in the class. We went out in the field, to Crown Point and other places. We looked at "outcrops" and noted the "striations" and calculated their geologic period.

The student assistant for my lab was Suzy Snyder, class of 1966. She was very pretty and wore skimpy denim short shorts. The other guys in the class and I followed her around like puppies and dutifully wrote whatever she said in our lab notebooks.

Third week in November, freshman year: We were in Geology lab in Warner Science, looking at rocks. Brew was called away. When he returned, it was obvious something was wrong.

"The President has been shot," he told us. "You may leave."

We quietly filed out and headed up to Proctor Hall where a TV was set up in the upstairs lounge. We spent most of the next week numbly watching the dramatic post-assassination events, crowded into that central campus space.

Un Americain Typique

I got a D in French my freshman year. I never worked so hard for anything in my life.

Passing an intermediate language course, or exempting out by testing, was also a graduation requirement. The intermediate sections were a dumping ground for many levels of ability and preparation.

There were eighteen students in my class at the outset. As soon as your performance flagged to a failing level, you were removed from the class. I'm serious. The assumption was if you're not getting it now, you'll never pass the next stage. It was like rent: miss a payment or two and you're evicted. Failure was common.

I knew there were two weaker and less confident students. They were quickly gone. The second half of the year-long course only had 12 students. I was one of them, hanging on by a thread.

We were permitted only two hours in the language lab in Hillcrest to make our weekly pronunciation tapes. I figured out when the sign-up sheet went up and signed on for many additional hours with pseudonyms: "Carl Yastrzemski" was often in the lab. I had to get a good grade on the pronunciation tapes because I invariably failed the weekly comprehension exercises (a scratchy tape of a DeGaulle speech or an interview with Jean Moreau).

Moreover, as an athlete, I would occasionally have to miss class for away games. I would approach Madame Vadon and in halting Francaise explain an upcoming absence.

"Bah," she sputtered in disgust. "Vous preferez des jeux frivoles!"

"Un americain typique," she called me.

It was not a compliment.

Frat Boy

When I came home for the Christmas holidays my sophomore year, I referred to the "guys at the House" in a conversation with my dad.

He said, "The guys at the House?"

"Yeah, the guys at the House, the fraternity."

"You joined a fraternity?"

"Yes, this fall"

"Why?"

"Why not? Everybody does. All the guys at Middlebury. That's the way we do it."

My dad deeply distrusted all purely social organizations, and believed the absence of frats at Bates was a credit to the institution.

"Everybody does it," he said. "That's a good reason."

The DU boys, 1966

"Mon Dieu"

I surrendered the longest home run in the history of baseball.

It was at West Point on our spring trip sophomore year, the first game I played for the Panther pastimers.

Tommy Clark, our best pitcher, started and got racked. I entered in the sixth or seventh inning, down a dozen or so runs.

I struck out the side in my first inning, then got the first two outs in the next. I was flying. Up came their clean-up hitter, an enormous basketball player named Mike Silliman.

I got two quick strikes on him, and then threw him my rinky-dink curve, as the situation demanded. I wanted it down in the strike zone, but missed, and it spun lazily to the plate about waist high. Silliman's eyes got big, and he took a mighty cut and hit the ball on a parabolic arc nearly out of sight.

It soared over the left field fence, still going up, landed in the distance taking a high bounce off the road which ran behind the fence, well behind the fence, and splashed into the Hudson River beyond.

Three days later the ball came ashore on a beach in Marseille. A French bather picked it up, exclaiming, "Mon dieu. Quest-ce que c'est?" I figure it traveled about 3000 miles.

I made that last part up, but the rest of it is true.

The pitcher with the fan, Butch Varno

Commitment

I fell in love in my junior year with my classmate, Anne Daignault.

We came from different backgrounds. Her family owned a beautiful apartment in Manhattan: Tower East, 32nd floor, East 72nd Street and Lexington. They also had a place on Cape Cod at Woods Hole.

When we started going out, I had never been to New York or Cape Cod. She was quite a catch: she had a car *and* a typewriter.

I went to Lewiston High School in Lewiston, Maine. She attended Concord Academy, a private girls school. My high school friends were the sons and daughters of millworkers.

She was an Art major, not into sports. Early in our relationship, she asked me if I would like to go to New York with her. "There's a new show at MOMA," she said, "and my parents are away."

I said, "Yes!" and then asked, "what's 'MOMA?'"

I quickly came to my senses, realizing I couldn't possibly get away. It was the middle of basketball season. "I have a game this weekend. I can't go to New York!"

"You have 25 games," she said. "Certainly you can miss one."

"I can't miss a game! I can't miss a *practice*."

She shook her head, "You cut class, but you'd never miss a basketball practice?"

This is an example of why coaches don't want their players to fall in love—at least not during the season.

Anne

Control Problems

Baseball coach Wendy Forbes was "old school." One of the greatest athletes ever to attend Middlebury, he did not inspire his players through positive reinforcement.

I was a pitcher. I threw hard and was prone to wildness. I walked batters. When this predilection got me in trouble,

Wendy beckoned to the umpire for "time out" and walked slowly to the mound.

"You tired?" he asked.

"No," I answered.

"Your arm hurt?"

"No."

"Well, throw the fucking ball over the plate," he advised, and left.

Wendy

Consolation

I drew the start against Dartmouth the spring of my junior year. They were very good, ultimately Eastern League Baseball Champs. We weren't. We were overmatched, and lost, 9–0, in a game that wasn't nearly that close. I went the whole miserable way, pitching all nine innings.

The Dartmouth pitcher one-hit us. I got the hit, a ground ball through hole into left. Small consolation.

Sometimes in sports, hard as you try, you realize the other guy is better than you are. There are no sentimental tales afterward of adversity overcome. In sports, sometimes you win, sometimes you lose, sometimes you get your ass kicked.

Anne's boyfriend in high school and for two years in college was a Dartmouth guy, the goalie on their hockey team. He was also President of the Beta fraternity, a jock house. After they broke up, she dated me.

When the Dartmouth frat boys heard that I was on the hill for the Panthers, they showed up *en masse* and rained abuse on me for three hours. The P.A. announcer, a student, was gleeful in describing the various manifestations of my inadequacy. It was a long afternoon. I never had a worse day in sports.

Late in the game, a pitch slipped from my hand and hit the Dartmouth batter, their shortstop, Mickey Beard (also their football quarterback). He already had three or four hits—the last thing I wanted to do was put him on base.

Nonetheless, he decided to charge the mound. I remember thinking, "Not only am I getting my ass kicked, but I'm going to get my ass kicked." Other players quickly intervened, and, as they say in sports, cooler heads prevailed.

Not much happened ultimately, but it kind of typified the day. The game mercifully ended and we dragged ourselves to the bus and the ride home.

Things improved when I got back home to Middlebury, as I was consoled by Anne.

Every once in a while the loser gets the girl.

Thirst

On a weekend when I was free, Anne invited me to New York to meet her parents for the first time.

They decided to have a small catered dinner party in my honor, eight people sitting around a table being served. Anne and I were by far the youngest. I was really nervous.

I declined the wine, the only beverage served. No way was I taking a chance drinking alcohol this night. I ate very little, carefully watching others, not wanting to make a mistake.

Finally, between courses, the server brought in small glasses of water. I was so thirsty I drank mine right down. Then I noticed the others were all daintily sticking their fingers in the water and wiping them off on their cloth napkins.

That's right. I drank the fingerbowl.

We didn't have fingerbowls in Lewiston.

Morning Glory

I loved writing for the *Campus*. Senior year my friend Rick
Hawley was the editor-in-chief; another friend Peter Lebenbaum
was the features editor; I was the sports editor and had inherited
a column, the "Inside Story," from Joe McLaughlin '65.

Monday and Tuesday were often all-nighters. We wrote our
articles and edited copy upstairs in Proctor Hall. I was slow, a
"hunt and peck," two-index finger typist (still am).

In the early morning hours, we took our copy to the Addison
Press downtown, to be returned as page proofs later in the day.
We often saw the dawn.

I'd go back to the dorm and crash, sleeping through my classes,
getting up for a sports practice in the afternoon.

I didn't let my studies get in the way of my extracurricular
activities. As a Dean, later, I gave good advice, from experience,
to students about managing their time.

"The Level of Sexual Intercourse"

By my junior year, Vietnam war protests were percolating and
students were getting restive. We particularly objected to single-
sex dorms. Tom Reynolds, who went on to be President at Bates,
was Dean of the College. Every so often, he held a State of the
College Address and Q & A.

At one of these sessions, in Mead Chapel, in the fall of my senior
year, 1966, Reynolds opened the proceedings by saying that
he had no interest "in raising the level of sexual intercourse at

Middlebury College" by introducing coeducation into the dorms. He went on to discuss dormitory architecture, observing that dorm rooms were essentially bedrooms.

The *Campus* quoted that remark in the lead of a page one story— and it became something of a catchphrase, open to ironic expression and various interpretations among students and faculty alike: "So, did you 'raise the level of sexual intercourse' last weekend, or what?" Comments like that.

Dean Reynolds was unhappy with this outcome and called Rick, the Editor, into his Old Chapel office and angrily asserted that he had been misquoted. Rick responded that we had taped the session and asked if he would like to hear the tape. "I certainly would," he responded.

We never got the tape back.

Dean of the College Thomas Reynolds

The Confession

We had only single-sex dorms in the 60s. When I arrived in 1963, freshmen women had to be in their dorms at 10:30 p.m. during the week and midnight on the weekends. After that, the doors were locked.

A girl arriving after the curfew had to ring a bell to get the House Mother to let her in: she got late minutes and had to face the dorm council and was often penalized by having an early curfew subsequent weekends. Unimaginable today. Repeated violations meant big trouble. Dean of Women Elizabeth Kelley, the custodian of the double standard, would simply dismiss you. *In loco parentis* was the rule.

Everything changed shortly thereafter, seemingly in a stroke, the result of student solidarity during the Vietnam War protests. Revolution is different from Evolution

Things were beginning to change when I was a student. The last two years, 1966–67, men and women were allowed five hours of visitation in one another's dorms on Saturday and Sunday afternoons, so called "parietal hours," under strict conditions (largely unenforced by student proctors). We won driving privileges for sophomores, yoo hoo.

My lifelong friend Gary Margolis was my roommate sophomore and junior years. We shared a suite on the fourth floor of Hepburn Hall as Junior Fellows. Sophomore year we lived on the first floor of Stewart, room 103 in the "Pits." The windows looked out, eye-level, to a grassy strip and road that circled the campus and the cemetery beyond. If we inadvertently locked ourselves out of our room it was easy get in the room through the window. We therefore never locked our window.

Sophomore year, Gary and I were on the basketball team and away from campus on weekend overnight trips for games on three occasions. Once when we returned from a hoop trip we both sensed something was awry in the room but couldn't identify anything specifically out of order. My bed smelled good—that was not usually the case. We thought nothing further of it.

In the week before graduation, our classmate Brian Bry approached us and said, "I have a confession. Sophomore year when you two played basketball I used to spend the weekend with my girlfriend from home in your room. We came in and out through the window." He added, "You guys really didn't keep a very clean room."

If we had known you were coming, Brian, we'd have picked up.

Grads Gary and Karl, 1967

Scotch Whiskey

It was May, junior year, and I was tired. The basketball season that winter had been long, only four victories. Then baseball too. After the Dartmouth fiasco (nine runs, 16 hits, six walks—lots of pitches), my arm was killing me. I started three more games, lost them all. I couldn't break a pane of glass with my fastball.

I was behind in my studies, overextended in my extracurricular life, and disappointed with myself for my choices. I would have to salvage the semester by another heroic burst at the end, night after night of all-nighters in the *Campus* offices. It was an exercise in self-disrespect.

It got so I couldn't sleep the night before an exam if I wanted to—I was so jazzed by coffee and anxiety.

So I went to see my academic adviser for some advice. I was toying with the idea of going to Bates, at home, for my senior year, get a fresh start of sorts, transfer those credits to my Middlebury degree, rid myself of my various extracurricular and social entanglements, be a conscientious student for once, escape, bolt, light out for the territories in my own limited cautious way.

I described my fatigue, and the Bates plan, and my adviser suggested we go for a hike that afternoon, drive up to Bread Loaf, relax, soak up the pastoral atmosphere, think deeply, talk.

Okay, I guess.

We hadn't walked far when he broke out a flask, scotch whiskey, and encouraged me to partake. It would relax me.

I had never tasted whiskey before. It was warm out and he suggested I take my shirt off. He took his off, not a pretty sight. He embraced me and kissed me.

I recoiled, repulsed. He retreated.

On the way back, he implored me not to tell anybody.

As soon as I got back to campus, I went to see Anne and we sat on the grass on the hill in front of Pearsons, her dorm. "You'll never believe what just happened to me," I told her. I told Gary and Rick and Peter too. It never crossed any of our minds to tell the authorities. What would they do? "What a creep," we thought, so reckless. It was an episode, a life lesson.

No permanent scars. The summer was restorative. I came back to Middlebury in the fall with renewed energy. I trusted people and was able to appreciate other male mentors along the way.

I changed advisers.

I hate the taste of Scotch.

Johnny America

Whenever I punched in at the factory, Pietro, one of my co-workers, led the men in greeting me: "Johnny America!" he shouted, and made the sound of pistols being fired, "kchoo, kchoo, kchoo," like a movie gunslinger.

Many of the workers were Italian, though the factory was in Switzerland in Brugg, about 25 kilometers from Zurich. Many had never met an American before. I was a cowboy, a symbol.

I got this off-the-books factory job by hook and by crook (my father knew somebody who knew somebody). I was looking for adventure, but my dad was not about to subsidize mere travel. Get a job, break even, pay your own way. I had spent the previous eight summers working at the Caddy Camp at the Poland Spring Hotel, a ten-week overnight work camp for boys, from Boston mostly.

I was 21, in my last summer before graduation, and ready for change. I had never flown in a plane before I got on Air France in June to Paris, with a connecting Swiss Air flight to Zurich.

I rented a room, bought a second-hand bike, and worked a nine-hour shift at the Georg Fischer Machinfabrik. Because of language issues, I was placed in the "transportation" section, loading and unloading trucks. I worked hard. I preferred being Johnny America to The Lazy American.

Nicola spoke a little French and translated for me, but mostly we communicated through gestures, sign language, and bonded by working side-by-side. I was a novelty and my relations with the other factory workers became, over time (I was there eight weeks) comfortable, even jocular.

They would often address me in their languages, Italian and Swiss-German, and were amused by my lack of comprehension. I took to telling them to "shut up" in mock exasperation.

They embraced the idiom and walked around telling one another to "shaddap, shaddap!"

So one day I asked Nicola "Comment on dit 'shut up!' en italien?" He thought for a minute and translated "shut up" as, "Va fungulo."

So the next time the opportunity presented itself, I told one of my co-workers who was ragging on me to "va fungulo." He was not amused. I realized immediately, from his baleful reaction, that the translation was not in the least precise.

Bye-Bye

Bayard Russ '66 was the only one of my contemporaries I knew who actually wanted to go to Vietnam. We called him "Bye-Bye," a prophetic nickname as it turned out.

When I was a student, Middlebury had compulsory Army ROTC for two years. After that, it was an elective. Many Middlebury men chose to continue and graduate as Second Lieutenants with a three-year military obligation. This decision sent them to Vietnam. While it's true that college boys mostly found ways to avoid service (the average age of soldiers in Vietnam was 19), it's not true of Middlebury boys.

Army ROTC was too tame for Bayard, so he enlisted in the Marine Corps Platoon Leader Course during his freshman year and spent two summers at Quantico in boot camp.

Bayard loved hard, physical work. My keenest memory is of him washing dishes in the frat house kitchen, apron around his torso, tossing things into the racks and the washer, steam all around, singing at the top of his voice like a wounded animal.

He was the goalie and captain of an undefeated soccer team in his senior year. Whenever he ran anywhere, on the practice field or on his own, he carried bricks in his hands to make them stronger. He signed letters to his friends, "Bayard 'What a Pair of Hands' Russ."

A Spanish major, he graduated in 1966 as a Second Lieutenant in the Marines and was ordered to the Defense Language Institute in Monterey to learn Vietnamese. In Vietnam, he was stationed for six months near DaNang, using his Vietnamese as an MP. He hated it—he wanted action, a platoon to lead. He wrote to a Middlebury friend, "I won't sit in the rear and mind the gear."

He got his wish. Barely. After only two weeks at the front, he was heading from DaNang to Khe Sanh when his unit was ambushed by North Vietnamese regulars (NVA). He was killed by a "hostile explosive device."

That was January 13, 1968. He had just turned 23.

January 13, 1968

LT. ALFRED BAYARD RUSS

Lt. Russ Killed in Action

Evaporation

Varsity Jim was a friend of mine. We were in the same fraternity. He wrote sports with me on the *Campus*.

Jim Allen was a big guy, a good football player, known for his ferocity on the field. His exuberance could be more off-putting than infectious to his teammates, one of whom said after a particularly enthusiastic outpouring, "Hey, *Varsity Jim*. Can it."

He was "Varsity Jim" thereafter, or "V.J." or "Veej." Such is the genesis of nicknames that stick. He took it all in good humor.

Varsity Jim went off the deep end in the late Sixties, absorbed by the radical anti-war protest movement. He quit school, read tracts, railed against the Establishment, and inhaled and ingested copious amounts of mind-altering drugs.

In the fall of 1968, he visited me at the boarding school where I was a first-year teacher. He arrived on an enormous motorcycle, dressed entirely in leather, curly hair down to his shoulders. My mind-blown students asked incredulously, "He's your friend?" My status with them was greatly enhanced, but I was quite sure I would not survive his visit employed.

I told him he could not smoke marijuana in my room in the dorm, so every couple of hours he zoomed off on his chopper and went for a ride, to commune with nature.

I asked him what he was doing with his life, and he said darkly, "blowing things up. You'll read about it."

Varsity Jim disappeared. His Middlebury girlfriend was the last to hear from him, on New Year's Eve, 1971. I have tried over the years to find out what happened to him, to no avail. He must be dead.

I went to the 25th reunion of his class at Middlebury and asked his classmates what they knew about Varsity Jim. One friend said, "I heard a long time ago that he was in prison in Arizona."

His best friend from college told me, "He evaporated."

Varsity Jim

Barnes Boffey

We were roused from our beds after midnight during Freshman
Orientation by the men in the Blue Key Honor Society, so that
we could serenade the senior women from the lawn in front of
Forest Hall. Freshman hazing required that we learn Gamaliel
Painter's Cane, the College Fight Song, and the Alma Mater.
I still know them.

My second night at Middlebury, with my little beanie on my head,
I stood behind the biggest person I had ever met, my classmate
Barnes Boffey, all 6'8" 300 pounds of him. I looked right into
the small of his back.

Possessed of a booming voice and an exuberant nature, he was
an original. He came to Middlebury from Williston Academy.
They had no football, so he played soccer there. I would have
liked to have seen him on the pitch.

Barnes was a presence. He presided in the Crest Room, the snack
bar in Proctor Hall. When he was glad to see me, he sometimes
just picked me up, growled "How ya doin'" and gave me a hug—
and I weighed 185 pounds. He majored in theater.

In his junior year he decided to go out for football. We all thought
it was a lark and figured he wouldn't last a week.

I was the Sports Editor of the *Campus* and met every Monday
morning with Athletic Director and football coach, the legendary
Duke Nelson.

He told me in his inimitable fashion about the confusion Barnes'
presence on the football roster caused when Duke sent

it to Wesleyan, the team's first opponent. Wesleyan saw a junior with an improbable name, "Barnes Boffey," who was listed at 275 pounds and 6'8". They sensed a practical joke—and were not amused.

The Wesleyan coach called Duke.

Duke told me, "Ba-Karl, Ba-Jeez son, they were really upset. I said to them, 'Ba-Coach, the boy's really out for the team.'" (Duke had a distinct speech mannerism: he started every utterance with the word "but.")

Turns out, with his size, Barnes was pretty good at football: courageous, immoveable. He played his senior year too.

After graduation, I went back to Maine to teach school and attend Army Reserve meetings. There, I made friends in the Reserves with a guy who played football at Bates and he asked me if I knew "Boffey, that big mean bastard."

"Barnes? He's a sweetheart."

In the spring of 1967, senior year, Barnes was drafted by the Pittsburgh Steelers and given a $1000 signing bonus which he spent buying beers for everyone at the Alibi.

He was cut after only a few days, but still . . . the Steelers!

*Barnes has worked with young people his entire professional life.
He is the Director of Training for the Aloha Foundation—
and was the longtime Director at Camp Lanakila in Fairlee, VT.*

Popcorn Problem

Barnes had ambivalence about his identity at Middlebury.
However, I had none. I remembered him in essence as a generous
and delightful person.

At our 25th reunion I told him that. He had chosen not to return to
Middlebury since graduation, though he lived in Vermont. He did
not want to reminisce about the good old days in college.

He earned a doctorate in education and became an alcohol counselor, working for a time at Dartmouth. While there, he helped make a video, "Fighting Drunk," that we used at Middlebury for years in our training of ResLife staff.

In it, Barnes made the point that students need to intervene when they see their classmates drinking excessively and dangerously. In training sessions with student leaders, I recited a wise analogy of Barnes's.

He posed this problem for us, on camera: "What if you had a roommate that was so fond of popcorn that every Friday and Saturday night he ate so much popcorn that he got sick, threw up.

"How long do you think it would be before you concluded he had a 'popcorn problem'?"

A Jungle in There

My lifelong friend and classmate, Jon Coffin, also felt deep personal ambivalence about his Middlebury past.

He believed that Middlebury had forsaken him when he was a student, not provided the support and concern that he needed at the time to succeed.

As with Barnes, I had no ambivalence about Jon. As a high school senior at Needham (MA), he visited Middlebury as a "prospective" the same weekend I did. We knew one another *before* we were classmates. He was the best man at my first wedding.

In the spring of 1968, after graduating, Jon and I traveled together for four months, hitch-hiking around southern Europe and northern Africa (Morocco). I had finished my active duty in the Army Reserve and Jon was about to head off for three years of military duty, ending up in Southeast Asia for a year.

He came home married to Panee, a Thai woman. He earned a M.A. in counseling, Panee earned a nursing degree, Jon went to work at the large public mental health agency in Burlington, they moved to South Hero on the Champlain Islands, and he and Panee had two children, Tahnthawan and Jaed.

When the marriage fell apart, Panee moved to Brunswick, Maine. Jon drove to Brunswick nearly every weekend. Tahnto attended St. Michael's and Jaed came to Middlebury.

Jon wrote in our 25th reunion notebook "I have chosen the inward journey — and found it to be a jungle in there."

Jaed, an extraordinarily talented student, had a positive experience at Middlebury. He graduated in 2002 Magna Cum Laude/Phi Beta Kappa, traveled the world, and became a writer. His first book, *A Chant to Soothe Wild Elephants*, did very well. It is the account of his year as a Buddhist monk in Thailand, his mom's home country. In 2015, all first-years at Middlebury read and discussed it in small groups.

I was invited to lead a discussion of Jaed's book that year. Jon came to our session and I introduced him as the father of the author. It was a thrill for both of us — and a treat for the students.

Jon chose a career in social work, specializing in alcohol counseling. He became the head of outpatient services at the Howard Mental Health Center in Burlington.

He described his method to me once as "balls to the walls." He specialized in the toughest cases, often taking on court-referrals, who either got into it with Jon and got better—or went to jail.

Jon's attitude about Middlebury softened over time, seeing it through Jaed's eyes. In 2012, he came to his 45th reunion and met his classmate Jana Holt, who, like Jon, had been married before. They didn't know one another as students. She was Janet Mara then, a skier and French major. They fell in love. They're married now, living in Brunswick, Maine, appreciative of Middlebury, and grateful they found one another.

Jon was fully deployed in the VT National Guard for the last 15 years of his career as a counselor and was the subject of a cover story in the Middlebury Magazine *for his work with soldiers returning from service in Iraq and Afghanistan.*

Danke Schoen

Jon and I have some wonderful memories, a few pictures, and a lot of stories about our hitch-hiking adventure in the spring of 1968 in Europe and North Africa. I offer just one here, but if you twist my arm, I could probably be convinced to tell a few more.

Our routine was to eat one meal, at night, and snack the rest of the day, pastries, fruit, bread, cheese. Our object was to save money—the less we spent, the longer we stayed.

We went from Luxembourg where Icelandic Airlines set us down, to Munich, for the beer (we were 23!), and also to check out a report we had heard along the way that an exporter of some kind was hiring footloose young guys—Europe was loaded with them in 1968—to drive Mercedes–Benz autos from Munich to Teheran to be sold on the black market there.

To a couple of hitch-hikers, the idea of driving a Mercedes anywhere was a dream come true. We investigated and what we discovered was really scary so we sensibly decided to go in a different direction, by train and by thumb: Italy, Southern France, Spain, Morocco—a Mediterranean odyssey.

One night while in Munich, we found a nice little restaurant whose bill of fare posted on the window outside accommodated our budget. We took our seats at a table next to a family of Americans, obvious from their conversation. Dad, mom, two or three kids, can't remember exactly.

We quickly became aware that whenever the waiter appeared with food or water, the father showed his appreciation by saying "donkey shit," with extravagant courtesy, an intentional mispronunciation of "danke schoen." Laughter all around.

This was 1968. Our war in Vietnam had not endeared Americans to our European friends. Jon and I had already felt a chilliness as young Americans abroad.

Every time this dad said "donkey shit," Jon got more upset. Finally, he could take it no longer. He was livid. He stood up to his full 6'2" height and his 225 lbs weight, walked deliberately over to the other table, bent over and got cheek to cheek with the dad, smiled broadly, and whispered, "if you say 'donkey shit' one more time to that waiter, I'm gonna beat the hell out of you, right in front of your family. Understand?"

Jon turned, smiled, and said to all, "Enjoy your meal."

Jon wouldn't have done it (I don't *think* he would have anyway), but believe me it was "danke schoen" after that, for the rest of the meal.

Jon and Karl board the Marrakech Express, Morocco, 1968

Weekend Warrior

As a student at Middlebury, I was required to take Army ROTC
for two years. After that, we could quit, and I did.

It was not a political or moral decision. I just hated the classes.
My favorite people growing up, role models and mentors, friends
of my dad, had been in the military in World War II.

I joined the Army less than two years after I quit ROTC, just
before my graduation. It was 1967 and the Vietnam War was
really heating up, and so were the student protests. I joined the
Army Reserves to avoid the War. Calling up the Reserves and
National Guard was politically impossible. They were safe
havens. The unit in Lewiston, my hometown, still had openings.

I was not brave enough to resist the draft, like my Middlebury
friend Dick Hall who went to Canada, or to make the decision of
my friend Bayard Russ who enlisted in the Marines.

I was grateful for this middle ground, but I worried it was a
coward's choice. I had been trained as an athlete to be brave
and loyal and obedient. General Eisenhower had said, "The true
mission of American sports is to train young men for war."
I bought it.

A week after I graduated I was in Fort Polk, Louisiana, for
Basic Training, where my "ass was grass," as Sneed Saunders,
a 6'6" drill sergeant, put it, and he was the "lawnmower."

I followed that with training as a medic at Fort Sam Houston
in San Antonio and then I came home to six years of part-time
training while pursuing a teaching career, a weekend warrior.

The weekend meetings were pitiful and Mickey Mouse, but I liked the two-week summer camps in hospitals and clinics (dispensaries). My first summer was at Camp Drum in upstate New York. I was on a ward of amputees, kids really, and my job was cleaning stumps, keeping infection at bay.

After that, my summer camps were at Fort Devens (MA), Fort Dix (NJ), Fort Storey (VA), and Fort Knox (KY).

I liked being a medic, wearing whites. I thought if teaching didn't work out, maybe I could be a nurse.

SDS Sneed Saunders
First Platoon

Not About Me

One of the most important lessons I learned about being a good dean I learned well before I actually became a dean at Middlebury in 1976.

My first teaching job was in Maine at a little boarding school, Kents Hill School, from 1968–70, tough years to be young. Kents Hill was only about 20 miles from Lewiston.

I spent a lot of time in Lewiston, playing basketball. Bates College has always been basketball-mad, and I got on their faculty and staff intramural basketball team as a "faculty child." I played with old high school pals in the Lewiston Rec League.

I went to Army Reserve meetings on Wednesday nights in Auburn, next to Lewiston, and made a couple of good friends from Bates College there.

Jim and I hit it off right away. He was my age, still in Lewiston teaching school because his girlfriend, Candy, was at Bates in 1969, about to graduate.

Candy fixed me up with her roommate and best friend, who was an outstanding student, a psychology major, headed for significant academic honors at graduation.

When I met her she was having trouble getting started on her thesis.

Our first date was a movie in Portland, Zeffirelli's "Romeo and Juliet"—what a good start. By spring, the thesis block was a full-blown crisis. She was getting lots of advice: "Just do it." "It doesn't have to be perfect." "Write something!"

I was confident I could help. My two-week spring vacation at Kents Hill coincided with hers at Bates. She moved into the empty dorm with me and set up her thesis materials at my desk. I would be so supportive, so nurturing, so attentive to her every need that the dam would break, her creativity would burst forth.

This was not hard duty for me. I was crazy about her. We went for rides around central Maine, and happened upon Eddie Lynch's wildflower field. We lazily followed a loon from a canoe on Lovejoy Pond. We spent a couple days at Boothbay Harbor in a room overlooking the haba.

None of it worked. When we returned to the desk and her books and yellow pads—no change. I remember standing helplessly by, watching her shoulders heave, hearing her sobs.

I realized *it was not about me.*

She had to figure out what was wrong, getting in the way, what the obstacle was. It was big and deep and I couldn't fix it.

She and I lasted a few years. We had some good times and some hard times. We went back and forth, but didn't make it, ultimately, together. For a while, I blamed the times, the Vietnam War, and all that came with it.

Our lives diverged. I moved to Cleveland, taught at a boys' school, wore a tie and jacket, went to weekend Reserve meetings and attended graduate school. I was cautious and practical.

She didn't graduate from Bates. She joined VISTA (the domestic Peace Corps: "Volunteers in Service to America"), and then lived on a commune in Thorndike, Maine, wore overalls, and learned carpentry. She was decidedly what we called then "counterculture." We married other people.

Bates left her graduation open-ended. It took her many years to finish.

Over the years I thought of her when I met with students who were unable to do their work, creatively paralyzed, blocked by emotional forces they couldn't identify or overcome. I knew that their problem didn't have to do with motivation, preparation, or effort.

I often made a deal with them. I'll intervene with your professor, I would say, do my best to help with your time issues, if you go to our counseling office and start to work on the sources of your paralysis, your block.

I liked using my office and authority to help students in distress, but I learned early on that my influence had limits and compassion alone was often not enough.

The Heist

On the spring day when I interviewed for the job at Middlebury, I went to lunch with Erica Wonnacott, dean of students, Dennis O'Brien, dean of the College, and Tim Carey, the assistant dean I would replace (he was headed off to Boston to teach at Noble and Greenough School, where he stayed, much beloved, for four decades).

We assembled at Erica's office in Old Chapel. "I'll drive," she volunteered.

There were only two seats in the cab of her truck, so she and Dennis got in the front. Tim and I climbed in the bed and sat on bales of hay. I had on a blazer and tie, my good pants, and man-shoes. Tim waved to some friends as we drove through town on the way to Fire & Ice.

At lunch, Dean O'Brien (soon to become the President of Bucknell) recounted his favorite Middlebury pranks. One had involved the liberation of the giant artificial plant everyone hated from the center of the snack bar (the Crest Room) in Proctor: Four hoods, dressed in wide-brimmed hats, dark glasses, zoot suits (from the St. Stephen's Church rummage sale) trained their plastic machine guns on the assembled throng at 10:00 p.m. when the snack bar was packed (freshmen women had a 10:30 curfew).

They told everyone to "freeze," unplugged the jukebox, then pushed the enormous planter out the door onto the Proctor patio to a thunderous ovation, and made their getaway. The *Campus* did a story on the heist.

I was presented with a dilemma. Do I tell them I was one of the four hoods, or would that mark me as not serious enough to be a dean? What the heck, I figured, I had just ridden to lunch on a bale of hay in the back of a truck.

I confessed.

I got the job.

So I came to Middlebury to become "Dean Lindholm" the same year, 1976, that my dad, "Dean Lindholm" at Bates, retired. I thought about naming a son "Dean," but my kids will have to become "Dean Lindholm" on their own.

Raft Race

Spring Weekend, my first year in the Dean's Office, 1977: my assignment for the Raft Race was to patrol in my car Three Mile Bridge Road, which runs adjacent to Otter Creek.

The Raft Race was an Erica Wonnacott innovation. Students built makeshift rafts from building materials they purchased (or frequently stole) and floated down Otter Creek from the Three Mile Bridge (no longer there) to the high school where they pulled out so as not to go over the falls. Erica and her husband Bruce (and a thermos of Bloody Mary's) were in a canoe at the end point, helping them out.

By no means was this a "race." It was more a continuation of a party from the night before. Students assembled their rafts in the early morning at the entry point, three miles upstream, and lay in provisions and accoutrements, which usually included a keg of beer, and maybe some food, and often a source of musical accompaniment—a boom box. If the current was too fast, they just tied up to a tree on the shore and partied. As I patrolled, I saw lots of students in the water. And plenty of drinking.

At our post mortems Monday morning, I said, "Erica, this is nuts! Somebody's gonna die. Drinking? On the water!"

She said, "Well, it's better than the Demolition Derby."

The what? The Demolition Derby. The previous three years had seen a Demo Derby, "organized" by the Sig Ep House (now Meeker House) on their front lawn. Mike Schoenfeld '73 proudly claims one year they had 21 old cars.

Not as bad as the Demolition Derby, maybe, but pretty bad.

The Raft Race only lasted another year or two before it was mercifully ended. There were still plenty of hijinks on Spring Weekend and yes, even some drinking, but nothing so organized as the Raft Race, except for maybe the Maypole Dance.

Director of Student Activities Jackie Flickinger, at someone's suggestion, decided we would have a Maypole Dance to kick off Spring Weekend. A tall pole was erected on the lawn outside Munroe with colorful ribbon cascading from the top.

At the appointed hour, accompanied by some recorded light classical music, many young women in white gossamer gowns would gambol around the pole weaving a beautiful pattern of colors, and Spring Weekend was officially underway.

A far cry from the Raft Race—and the Demo Derby.

Erica

Naked Truth

The Deans had to conduct dorm inspections. These were
pre-announced, but we still found our share of contraband.

We broke up into teams—one student affairs staff member, the
R.A. of the dorm (then called the House Director), and someone
from Facilities—Buildings and Grounds in those days.

Jackie Flickinger had been shocked during her dorm inspection
a few days earlier when she knocked on a door, was invited
to "come in," and was greeted warmly by three entirely naked
students. She quickly left, and shortly thereafter informed Erica
that she would no longer be doing dorm inspections.

Being new, I was shadowing the associate dean, Arnold
McKinney, on a late afternoon inspection of Hepburn Hall.
An African-American, Arnold was in charge of our diversity
programs, extensive in this decade after the assassination of
Martin Luther King Jr., as well as serving generally as a Dean.

Arnold was a couple years younger than I, but we knew one
another as schoolmates and I consider him one of my mentors
in the dean business. He left after that year, 1977, to go to
divinity school at Morehouse, became a minister, led a church in
Waycross, GA (a long way from his home in the South Bronx),
and died too young, in 1996, at 49.

We knocked on the door of a fourth floor triple in Hepburn. "Just
a minute," the inhabitants instructed, then said, "Okay. Come
in." Just inside the door, straight ahead was a bunk bed. On the
top bunk, two students faced us, a couple, male and female, their
legs dangling over the bed. Keen observer that I am, I noticed
immediately they had no clothes on. It was a full frontal assault.

I was taken aback. Arnold was not.

Unperturbed, he strolled about the room, casually looking things over, asking questions: "How's the heat? Radiators work? The windows tight? Do you have any candles? They're not allowed, you know." He made sure they had no flammable tapestries on the wall and the sprinkler heads were free of adornment.

Then he came back to the bunk beds, and stood directly in front of the students, and further engaged them in conversation, asking about their majors, backgrounds, and so on.

It wasn't long before they dived under the covers in embarrassment, and we left.

Arnold was cool.

ARNOLD McKINNEY
Assistant Dean of Students

The Wrong Folk

Arnold and I drove over to Bates College where he spoke to their student affairs staff about minority students on campus and their needs. At other colleges intent on diversifying their student body, Arnold had developed something of a reputation as a sage.

He made a number of suggestions as to the ways Bates could provide for this new constituency, help make them feel welcome on their campus. He talked about the importance of everything from hair care to the need for academic support and new initiatives in admissions recruiting.

He reflected on music and cultural preferences: "There's nothing wrong with folk music," he said. "It just appeals to the wrong folk."

He added, "Black students don't listen to John Elton."

On the way home, I said, "Arnold, his name isn't John Elton. It's Elton John."

"I know, Karl," he said.

Jack Daniels

Arnold was a night person and an insomniac. He loved to go out and did, virtually every night. Once or twice a week he'd drive up to Burlington to a dance club with live music. The housing intern, Jill, was always game. Sometimes my wife, Jody, would go too. Early in the evenings he and his wife, Karen (Smallwood, class of '74), entertained students of color in their home, a College rental on South Street. Arnold cooked; his specialty was fried chicken.

The place to go in downtown Middlebury in 1977 was Fire & Ice. It had the liveliest bar scene and live music some nights (I heard Richie Havens and John Sebastian there). It was a fun place. There was alcohol involved. The legal drinking age was 18.

My wife of two years, Jody, and I lived only a block away on North Pleasant Street (Route 7 North). Arnold called most nights and asked if I wanted to meet him at Fire & Ice about 10:00 p.m.

I'd have a few beers, stay out late, and show up to work the next day, dragging. Not Arnold. He would arrive chipper, dressed formally as always, in a suit with a vest, or a sport coat, tie, and slacks.

I finally realized he wasn't drinking. He would order a Jack Daniels on the rocks, and maybe, rarely, a second. He nursed that drink for hours. He was out to socialize, not to drink.

I was not a sophisticated drinker. I once asked Arnold what the difference was between Bourbon and Scotch.

He told me: "White people who live in suburbs in Connecticut drink Scotch. Black people drink Bourbon,"

Good enough for me.

Arnold and Karen back at Middlebury, 15 years later

An American Academic

Jody and I were walking near Harrod's in London when a very tall man and attractive lady passed us.

"Know who that is?" I asked her.

"No."

"That's Kurt Rambis of the Lakers," I said confidently.

She rolled her eyes. "Karl. Every tall guy is not a professional basketball player. We're in London. Give me a break."

This was not a difficult call for me. The Lakers had just won the NBA Championship and I'd watched all the games. Rambis was a prominent player who wore distinctive black-rimmed glasses.

We were in London on a study-abroad trip—I was overseeing from the Dean of Students Office non-Middlebury study abroad. In this role, I became a member of the Board of Advisers at Beaver College's Center for Education Abroad. Beaver had a number of programs in the U.K. and sent its board there every other year. We had an afternoon free of meetings and Jody and I were walking London's shopping district.

"No, seriously," I insisted, "that's Kurt Rambis."

"Right."

I took her hand and we caught up to the Rambis-lookalike, strolling with his lady, window-shopping. I approached and said confidently, "Kurt! Congratulations on the Championship."

The big man turned and gave us a smile. "Hey, thanks a lot."

It was indeed Rambis. He appeared glad to see a countryman. "What are you doing here," he asked warmly. "We're here for Wimbledon. Don't you love London?"

I was flustered, tongue-tied, unprepared for an actual conversation. All I had intended was to show Ms. Smarty-Pants that I knew what I was talking about. I mumbled that I was an "American academic," in London for meetings. I then beat a panic-stricken retreat. "Nice to meetcha."

That's the best you could come up with?" Jody said, "You're an '*American academic*'"?

After that encounter, on that trip—and on innumerable occasions after that, Jody introduced me as "my husband, Karl. He's an 'American Academic.'"

Innocent Abroad

Then there was the time I left my pants in the Hotel Continental in Florence, or so I thought.

I was traveling to Italy and France with Middlebury's Vice President for Languages Ed Knox, getting to know our schools in Florence and Paris, visiting with students.

I tried to pick up a little useful Italian while in Florence, but the only word I remember now (other than "ciao") because I used it so often was "ricevuta," which translates to "receipt."

Traveling for the College, you can be sure whenever I paid a bill or made a purchase I said, "ricevuta, per favore."

"Grazie!"

Anyway, the pants.

Our program in Italy was directed by an art historian Anna Barsanti, an elegant woman some years my senior.

When I got to Paris, I couldn't find my pants, and they were my suit pants, not just a regular of pair of pants. I only owned one suit, so I was reluctant to part with those pants.

In dismay, I told Ed of my pants problem and he said he would contact Anna, who would take care of the matter and have the pants sent to me forthwith.

To this day I think with embarrassment of the dignified Professora Barsanti going to the hotel and inquiring about "il pantaloni" of the American from Middlebury.

Ed told me that Anna had reported that they scoured my room at the hotel, and, alas, found no pants.

Some months later I found them in my suitcase in a compartment I had forgotten even existed.

This was the new suitcase I had purchased at the New Hampshire Mall on my way to Boston to catch the plane for this trip. I was unfamiliar with all of its pockets.

My old one was destroyed when I accidentally backed my car over it in my driveway in East Middlebury in my haste to get on the road to the airport on this trip.

"Che imbecille!"

Captain von Trapp

Parents Weekend, the early 1980s: Jody and I were with friends for dinner at Mister Ups, sitting in a booth in the back room.

A family was escorted to the booth behind ours. I recognized the voice of the woman in the group of three. It was the distinctive purr of the actress Tammy Grimes, whose daughter, Amanda Plummer (a well-known actor in her own right), was a Middlebury student.

I told Jody that celebrities of sort were sitting in the booth next to us. Then I added, "Christopher Plummer is Amanda's dad. I wonder if he's with them."

Jody was thunderstruck. "He is!" she gasped. "It's *him*." And there he was, just a few feet away.

I wasn't aware that the film "The Sound of Music" was a favorite of Jody's growing up and Captain von Trapp was her ideal man. She was in a daze the whole meal.

You'd have thought Larry Bird himself were in the next booth.

The "H" is Silent

In my sports fandom, I am partisan and excitable. I used to be worse.

I have the same affliction, more or less, as most graduates of NESCAC schools—can't stand Williams or Amherst for their smug superiority (okay, okay, their continued excellence). I have a bigger problem with Amherst, as a couple of my best friends after college were Williams guys.

I had a roommate from Amherst when I was teaching in Cleveland. At a party one night, I introduced him to a friend, "This is Pete, my housemate, he's from Amherst." Pete felt the need to correct me, saying, "Karl, the 'h' is silent. It's pronounced 'Am - erst.'"

After that, whenever I said "Amherst," especially in his presence, I became Sean Connery and exaggerated the second syllable: "am – HHHHHHurst," like a Scotsman. He cringed every time.

In my second year as a young dean, I attended a Middlebury–Amherst basketball game in our gym, with maybe 50–100 other fans, the usual sparse crowd. My friend Russ Reilly had come to Middlebury from Bates to be our basketball coach.

The score was tied as the time wound down in the first half. Amherst took an errant shot as time expired, 0:00 on the clock, only no buzzer went off ending play. The scoreboard operator at the table had forgotten to switch on the "automatic horn." Amherst took another shot, missed, and then hit a tip-in, before the officials realized time had run out and blew their whistles.

I was not alone in loudly protesting this miscarriage; everyone was screaming "Clock! Clock! as the Jeffs were rebounding their missed shots.

I was alone, however, in marching down from my seat in the stands to the vicinity of the scorers' table where coaches and officials were huddling. My contribution to the discussion was to scream, "DON'T COUNT THE HOOP!" and to offer other such protestations, amounting to the same thing. There was no need at all for discussion, it seemed to me.

As they dithered I turned my attention to the Amherst coach and insisted that he should acknowledge the hoop shouldn't count. "C'mon, Coach, you know it was late, don't take the hoop." Then I became sarcastic, "You're Am-erst (note: no "h"), after all. The mighty Amherst. Don't take the basket. Do the right thing! Sportmanship!"

The Amherst coach, only 10–15 feet away from me, looked right at me. I didn't back off. I yelled at him, "Yeah, I'm talking to you, Coach. You know it was late. Show some class! Am-erst!"

The refs counted the hoop and the teams and officials left the court, and I was left standing there with my pants down, so to speak. I was embarrassed by my outburst. Humiliated would not be an exaggeration. Trust me, it was a bad performance.

I immediately left the building and went home. I sat down and wrote a letter of apology by hand to the Amherst coach, and drove it to the post office that night and deposited it in a mailbox there.

A couple days later, I got a letter in the mail, the return address of which was "Athletics, Amherst College, Amherst, MA." It was from the Amherst coach. Our letters had crossed. He had clearly asked somebody who that maniac was yelling at him.

He rightfully took me to task, asking how a dean could be such a poor model for his students, and so on. It was a difficult letter to read, but he had a point.

I wish I had saved his letter now. I can't remember its precise content. He earned my grudging respect with it: he had written this letter to me, no copies to the Middlebury President or Dean of the College, my bosses. His quarrel was with me.

I spoke to Erica, the dean of students, and to John Spencer, the dean of the college, describing my behavior. They did not overly chastise; in fact, they seemed mildly amused.

However, they were not there at the game.

I have been better behaved at basketball games ever since then, even close games with Amherst.

We lost that game by two points. You can look it up.

Not Guilty

Erica Wonnacott was notoriously liberal of second (and third) chances. The wonderful Frank Kelley, too.

Frank arrived in 1985, after 25 years teaching Latin and serving as Principal at Middlebury High, to be our first Director of Residential Life. He once said to me about student misbehavior: "fool me once, shame on you; fool me twice, shame on you; fool me *three times*, shame on me."

Erica was hard on girls and forgiving of boys, knowing what essentially flawed creatures they were (we are). I tried to convince her that some boys, only a few to be sure, were thoroughly incorrigible, rotten apples, and deserved to depart, but she didn't believe me. She thought all boys could be redeemed, and she redeemed more than a few.

What I learned from being a part of so many discipline cases that went to judicial hearings was that often there's a world of difference between "Not Guilty" and "Innocent."

What "not guilty" often meant in our microcosm, as in the real world, is we can't prove your guilt. And in colleges, especially back then, we did not have many investigative advantages.

For a long time we allowed students who were charged with a serious breach of respect or appropriate behavior the choice between a jury of their peers—an all-student panel of nine members, or a panel of three or four Deans of Students.

This was conceived in the 1960s by newly empowered students. It broke down in the 1980s and 1990s because the overwhelming choice of students, often after consulting with parents, was to be heard by the deans, believing they would receive a more consistent application of justice. So much for student solidarity.

Dean Ann Hanson wisely put together in the 1990s a community judicial board, broadly composed, and had it vetted by various groups, and that remains our approach today.

I know we let off with no punishment students who were guilty of crimes and misdemeanors because we couldn't be sure of their guilt, even though we held ourselves to a different evidentiary standard: ours was a "preponderance of the evidence."

The hardest were sexual misconduct cases. One party says coercion; the other claims consensual sex. Both parties' memories are dulled by drink. No witnesses.

It's hard to kick a student out of school with no possibility of return (which is what a guilty verdict would demand for a date rape or sexual assault, for example), usually a young man in these cases, because you're *pretty sure* he did it. And the victims want and expect justice from us because they have even less confidence in the local police and criminal justice authorities and their processes, whom they have chosen not to engage.

To be honest, I was always grateful that when we (the deans) heard sexual misconduct cases, the panel included three women and one man, me. The presence of women at least reassured at the outset that the deck was not stacked against female victims.

It's different now. Sexual misconduct on college campuses has been recognized as the serious problem that it is and has been for a long time—and is being addressed in a variety of ways. Middlebury has a dean who works almost exclusively on sexual assault cases—and another dean (both women) whose job is to handle student conduct matters.

Deans cannot have "private" conversations with students about matters of sexual misconduct: they are required by law to report any information, however preliminary. We hire outside investigators for follow-up.

Lawyers now can attend our judicial hearings. It's a very formal process.

Times change.

Slug Barn

I hated Winter Carnival. If you asked me to list the ten most unpleasant things I had to deal with as a dean, all ten would be from Winter Carnival. Actually twelve or thirteen of the ten worst things maybe.

One year, Jody's sister and her husband were visiting from Maine on a Carnival Weekend, sleeping on the foldout couch in our living room. They came to watch the skiing.

I got a call well after midnight on Friday from Security asking for my help in closing a big pajama party at Hillcrest (now Franklin Environmental Center). I tried to be quiet as I left home but my sister-in-law, Jane, woke up. "Where are you going at this hour?" she asked.

"Work," I whispered.

"Nice job," she said.

Another year, just as I had come home from the raucous Late Night Club in Upper Proctor, I got a call from Campus Security that the Slug party wouldn't close. The neighbors were livid and the town police were on the scene.

The "Slug" house (Alpha Sigma Psi), called Fletcher these days, held their parties in the big barn adjacent to the house, now used for storage. The band played downstairs and students danced (there was some drinking too, as hard as that is to believe) upstairs.

You could see the upstairs floor swaying from the dancers' collective weight. To get there, party-goers had to climb a wooden ladder. I'm surprised no one was ever injured in a fall.

When I arrived, I tried to find the house President amid the 100–200 revelers. When I found him, I told him the party had to close. He said, "Okay. Last song," whereupon the band played a 45-minute last song.

I found him again and insisted the music cease, the party close, or there would be "consequences."

So he took the mike and said, "the dean is here and says we must close the party down."

At this point, a chant erupted from the throng upstairs:

"FUCK THE DEAN, FUCK THE DEAN, FUCK THE DEAN!"

Someone poured a pitcher of beer down from above, intended for me I'm quite sure, but it drenched instead the Campus Security officer standing next to me.

He quit the next day. I stayed on for another twenty-five years.

Fletcher House these days, with the adjacent storage facility, once the Slug (Alpha Sigma Psi) House and Slug Party Barn.

Shafted

Being the only male (with ten women) in the Dean of Students office for many years, I was called on whenever there was a fraternity outrage—that is, about every weekend.

This was one of the most egregious. It combined the frat wars *and* Winter Carnival.

The frats were furious with us. A broadly composed committee on Student Social Life, had determined that the Comprehensive Fee and fraternity dining couldn't coexist. So the Committee recommended the elimination of fraternity dining. The frats, with justification, considered dining their lifeblood.

Cut to Winter Carnival 1979. Buildings and Grounds deposited a large pile of snow in front of all the dorms and fraternities for the traditional exercise of making snow sculptures.
Who knew the Delta Upsilon fraternity had such artistic ability?

The DU guys sculpted a large, 15-foot high penis, surrounded by a hand, four fingers and a thumb. A very realistic rendering. Unmistakable. At the base, they molded the word, "Shafted."

In the Dean's Office, we temporized. Sometimes when you intervene, matters get worse. If you are in authority and you back off, students can lose interest, things cool off, life goes on.

Or not.

The DU snow penis quickly became a tourist attraction. People drove from as far away as Burlington to take pictures. Cars lined up on Main Street. There was a buzz in the town.

Trustee and Middlebury benefactor John Kirk (of Kirk Alumni Center) lived in Cornwall and was apoplectic when he drove by and saw the crowd of onlookers. He stormed into President Robison's Office and demanded an end to this embarrassment.

The President asked the Dean of the College, John Spencer, to take care of the matter, get rid of the sculpture. John called me. We made a plan and contacted Middlebury town officials, who

ry College, Middlebury, Vermont   February 28, 1979

School bulldozes sculptures

By SANDRA MURRAY

Snow sculptures created by DU and Chi Psi fraternities succumbed to bulldozers commissioned by the administration last Friday morning, Feb. 23.

According to Dean of the College John Spencer, the College received calls from the Middlebury Board of Selectmen, the School Committee, the local and state police and hundreds of townspeople complaining that the sculptures were "obscene and disgusting."

Dean of Students Erica Wonnacott asked DU to take down their snow sculpture, "Shafted," the evening of Feb. 22, but was ignored. The next morning, Spencer and Karl Lindholm, assistant dean of students, went over to both fraternities, asking them to consent to the removal of the sculptures at the expense of the College.

DU members, who ask not to be identified, said Lindholm and Spencer warned them that if they did not take the sculptures down, or allow them to be taken down, the town of Middlebury would

Lindholm that the Middlebury town council had held an emergency meeting regarding the snow sculptures. That Council, the deans said, voted to press charges against the fraternities if the sculptures were not removed from their front lawns as soon as possible.

Findlay said that after hearing about the town council's threats, Chi Psi was ready to take its sculpture, "Half Moon," down, but the College had already arranged to do so. Across the street, DU was more adamant about its position. "We let them

take it down. We weren't going to do it ourselves," said the DU members.

As for disciplinary action on the part of the College, Findlay said he is sure nothing will happen to Chi Psi, even though the political overtones of the sculpture were aimed (literally) at Old Chapel. DU is not so sure that they will escape the administrative wrath. One DU member explained the implications of their snow sculpture, "It was made for the purpose of letting students know that fraternities have been shafted by the administration."

agreed to send an earthmover to the frat house the next morning at a designated time to knock down the sculpture.

Early Saturday morning, John and I set out to do our duty. He looked like a faculty member from Central Casting: tweed sport coat, crew neck sweater, scarf, charcoal gray slacks, L.L. Bean boots. I was a Yankee Sancho Panza—jeans, sweatshirt, jacket, blue watchcap. We went into the DU house (now the Health Center) to wake up the President. We gave him a story about the town bringing "indecent exposure" or "disturbing the peace" charges against the House. A fabrication, but not far-fetched. We said we would do him the favor of taking down the offending representation.

We then went and stood by the giant snow penis and waited for the heavy equipment to arrive, and twiddled our thumbs. I don't think I have ever felt so dumb and exposed.

Soon enough, a giant, many-ton earth mover, the praying mantis kind, lumbered up Main Street. It was way more machine than the job required.

The operator knew exactly what to do. BOOM, down went the DU penis. The DU boys, assembled in front of their house in their jammies and bathrobes, let out a huge cheer.

The earth mover turned and rumbled back down Main Street.

Mission accomplished, John and I went out for coffee.

Calm in Crisis

The burning of Recitation Hall, the ROTC building, in 1969 has become something of a Middlebury myth, a bizarre badge of honor and palpable example that we too had the anti-war protest chops, like others across the country—Berkeley, Harvard, Kent State, Columbia, Wisconsin, with well-publicized disruptions.

Dave Nicholson '67 wrote in his Vietnam memoir that "anti-war activists" burned the ROTC building "to the ground." In fact, it was burned to a shell, but had such extensive interior damage that it was declared a "total loss." It was torched four days after the Kent State shootings, during a week of inflamed passions.

I was not at Middlebury at the time, but Erica Wonnacott was. She often reflected that the arson was the act of a solitary troubled student. He was responding to the impassioned rhetoric of the moment, in an attempt to ingratiate himself to his anti-war schoolmates, who were of course horrified by this gesture.

Recitation Hall after the fire:
exterior—a shell; interior—a total loss

She would tell the story when she feared that emotional rhetoric of the moment ran the risk of encouraging regrettable action. There can be unintended consequences, she warned.

The building's destruction came in Erica's second year at Middlebury, her first as the first Dean of Students. She had been Assistant Dean of Women under the legendary Elizabeth Kelly. "Ma" Kelly saw the deluge about to hit and wisely retired after more than two decades holding the fort against change.

I was elsewhere in the years between my graduation in 1967 and my return in 1976, but I am certain that Erica's calm in crisis, her constant equanimity, the confidence she had in her instincts was accounted for by the trial by fire of her first years.

Zorro

I *was* there about a decade later when Chaplain Scott took a cream pie in the face at a Commencement ceremony.

The pie was intended for President Robison but Charlie stepped in and took one in the squash. It was supposed to be funny, a prank, but not a soul was amused. It was frightening.

For a long time, Commencement was held outside on the greensward behind Forest Hall, extending onto Battell "beach." The principals would sit on a large stage, extending out from the elegant portico on the backside of the dorm.

The President was making some formal remarks early in the ceremony from the lectern at the front of the stage, when this figure dressed like "Zorro," head to toe in black, with a cape and gaucho hat, dashed from behind the assembled family and friends through the center aisle and up onto the stage.

Everyone was transfixed in the moment, seconds really. No one had any idea what his intent was, but all feared the worst.

I was seated in the audience, on the Battell side, and immediately got up and "raced" around the east side of Forest with the intent of, what . . . catching this guy?

It was obvious that his escape route would be through the startled dignitaries on the stage and through the glass doors into Forest East Lounge and out the front door of the building.

The problem with my quick thinking was that my effort was absurd: I had just had knee surgery and was on crutches and in a cast from toe to hip. I "hobbled" as quickly as I could around

the side of the building. I did indeed get a look at Zorro coming out the front door of Forest East, crossing College Street and sprinting around Munroe across the quad to a waiting car in front of Old Chapel, doing the 100-yard dash in about four seconds. He was flying.

No terrible harm ultimately, beyond embarrassment and fright. Erica later found out who did it—the student confessed and was summarily dismissed. She told me later that he came back eventually and graduated. This was all done quietly. She never told me who the culprit was—and I didn't ask.

After that drama at Commencement, we hired a student to sit next to the diplomas on stage as security. He wore a black robe like everyone else and just sat there unobtrusively. That was my idea and I picked the student each year for as long as I was in the Dean's Office. I prepared him by telling him the Zorro story and said his job if anyone rushed the stage was to tackle him.

I always selected a defensive back from the football team because those guys are tough and fast and not distractingly large—and they can tackle!

Forgiven

Andy McCabe, class of 1983, was such an interesting guy. When he was a student, he would on occasion stop in at the Dean of Students Office just to chat. A philosophy major, he loved discussion and debate, even then.

After graduation, he joined the Peace Corps in the Philippines. He married a schoolmate and eventually settled in Middlebury, where they raised their three kids.
Andy was an oenophile and opened wine shops in Middlebury and Vergennes.

He loved soccer and served for eight years as Dave Saward's top assistant at Middlebury before becoming head coach at Bard College in 2013. Bard and Andy were a perfect match of quirkiness and love of sport.

My son David, Middlebury 2005, is absorbed professionally with soccer, having worked in Major League Soccer (MLS) in Los Angeles and Denver for eight years. In 2007, he and Andy were assistant coaches when the Panthers won the National Championship.

Andy was struck dead at 54, heart attack, in the spring of 2016. Over 400 people attended his memorial service in Mead Chapel, the whole Middlebury soccer community from the last 30 years. The entire Bard team came from Annandale-on-Hudson, NY, to honor their charismatic and eccentric coach.

The afternoon of the April service over 75 players hit the Middlebury pitch for a couple of hours of pick-up soccer.

That night, the Middlebury soccer alums repaired to the watering holes in town to celebrate their passion for soccer and Middlebury that they all shared.

David met many of his soccer elders. The next day, he visited us in Cornwall and reported to me, "They forgive you, Dad. They know you had a hard job."

"Thanks, Dave."

I am endorsed by my kids.

David, the goalie, 2003

The Commissioner

About 11:30 one morning I got a call on my extension from Jody, who worked in admissions at Middlebury. She had worked for my dad in admissions at Bates—that's how we met (my dad married us) and she worked with Fred Neuberger—and Bert Phinney, Carolyn Perine, Barbara Marlow, and other wonderful people at Middlebury for nearly ten years.

"Karl," she said, "There's a family visiting today and I hope you will take them to lunch."

I was frankly annoyed. "Jody, this is a busy day for me. Can't you do it or find someone else?" I asked, huffily.
"Okay, I'll tell the Commissioner of Baseball you don't have time."

"The who?"

"I interviewed Stephen Kuhn this morning—and I told him and his parents that you, a dean, might have some time for them."

I told her I would find the time.

We went to Fire & Ice. Baseball Commissioner Bowie Kuhn had reputation as a stiff and formal man—and he was that, but in this setting he was personable and engaging. I was on my best behavior and took care not to just pump him about baseball issues. I talked about Middlebury and was sure to include Stephen and his mom in the conversation.

That very morning, in the lobby of the Middlebury Inn that morning, Commissioner Kuhn had bumped into Hall of Famer, Ralph Kiner, famous player and long-time Mets announcer, who was visiting Middlebury with his daughter, Kimberlee.

We must have done something right—they both came to Middlebury and graduated in 1983.

Rugby Daffodils

The Rugby Team was always in trouble.

In fact, I think they were actually disappointed if they completed a season without being suspended for some outrage or another.

Rugby was a "club" for a long time, funded by the Student Activities Fee and outside the purview of the Athletic Department. Rugby players liked being outlaws. The players take great pride in their hardiness: their cars and trucks sport a bumper sticker that says, "It takes leather balls to play rugby."

Generally, rugby games ended and the parties began, with lots of drinking and singing of bawdy songs, and lots of drinking. A lot of drinking. Did I mention there was drinking after games?

We once received a midweek letter from the Dean at Colby College describing in detail the nocturnal outrages of our rugby boys the previous weekend. They were positively identified by their garb, their Middlebury sweats.

I proposed to buy them all sweatshirts that read "Williams College" to wear at their post-game revels on the road, but Erica had an even better idea: she imposed a work component to their penalty. She required them to plant daffodil bulbs at various locations around the campus. She supervised this effort herself.

Now, every spring, in front of Old Chapel, for example, and beside the sidewalk between Munroe and Gifford, these lovely harbingers of spring blossom and raise everyone's spirits.

They are the Rugby daffodils.

Erica and President Olin Robison

Geraldine

Winter Carnival, 1986: I had been on campus until late supporting Campus Security at the Klondike Rush concert in the field house. At 4:00 a.m. I was awakened from sleep at home by a ringing phone.

Now what?

It was Geraldine Ferraro calling from Hawaii. Her son, John Zaccaro, was a senior at Middlebury. A little more than a year before, Ferraro and Walter Mondale had lost the Presidential election to Ronald Reagan and George H.W. Bush.

I was the Middlebury liaison to the Zacarro family. During the Presidential election, John had taken time off to help his mother's campaign. I met with the family on a number of occasions to plan the details of his comings and goings.

The night of Rep. Ferrero's call, John had been arrested at his off-campus apartment for selling cocaine to an undercover police officer. His nickname among students, we learned later, was "the Pharmacist."

Coincidently, his apartment was the same one Jody and I had rented my first year working at the College.

Ms. Ferraro told me she had just been on the phone with "Madeleine" (that would be Gov. Madeleine Kunin) who had recommended the "best lawyer in the state" (Charles Tetzlaff, former U.S. Attorney from Vermont).

She closed her conversation with me with, "I'll be in touch."

"I bet," I said to myself, back in bed, wide-awake. "This is going to get interesting," and it certainly did.

Overmatched

I was dispatched by the President to meet with the Zacarro family to discuss the College's response to John's arrest. The President's Staff had decided that it would be best if he withdrew from Middlebury while the case was being adjudicated. I knew the family, so I was to deliver this message.

We met at the President's House. Media, reporters from all over, had assembled in the town, staking out the Middlebury Inn, and we thought this location presented the best place to escape attention.

So we assembled at 3 South Street.

After exchanging strained pleasantries, we all sat down at the dining room table and I laid out the College's position.

I was as overmatched as I had been at the Dartmouth baseball game years before.

"Not even close, Dean" Ms. Ferraro said, after I had laid out the College's plan for John's withdrawal. "He is going back in the dorm to work on his thesis and be a perfect angel," she said, while his case was being settled in the local courts.

The Zacarro's argument was that John had been targeted for "selective prosecution," that the College and town were out to get him, the son of a public figure, for its own purposes. Their strategy was to delay the actual trial as long as possible with legal maneuverings.

After eight months of observing the convolutions of the judicial system in town, we charged John with "conduct unbecoming," or some such, and scheduled our own hearing.

As we expected, John did not appear—our proceedings are not protected, thus subject to subpoena. He withdrew from school instead, "charges pending."

This result ultimately did not provide much of an impediment to John, as he was able to earn his undergraduate degree from Hunter College and a law degree from Catholic University.

Eventually, two years after his arrest, he was tried in town, found guilty of selling cocaine, and served four months of "house arrest," in a nice apartment in Burlington ("Thanks, Mom") and allowed to work a soft job.

In the aftermath, Geraldine Ferraro stuck it to Middlebury College and the hick town that abused her boy whenever she had the opportunity, in speeches, in print, and on TV.

I had voted for her, but in the end I didn't like or respect her much.

Hugging

Erica called me in her office and told me about the meeting she had just had with a female student, who told her of an encounter with one of her teachers, a well-known writer who was in residence at Middlebury for the year.

An aspiring writer, she had gone to his office to discuss her recent work. Much of her writing was of a personal sort as she tried to translate personal pain into art.

She cried. The writer rose to console her and hugged her. Very quickly, she said, his touch became inappropriate. He had gone too far, he "molested" her.

She came to see Erica because she wanted to get out of the course, and it was after the deadline to do so. Understandably she didn't want to return to the class. She was up-to-date in her work and was getting a good grade. She just wanted out. She didn't want to ever see him again.

Erica asked me to go see the writer, and explain what he had been accused of doing. See what he had to say. This was not easy for me. I had no personal relationship with the writer, but had read and admired his work.

He told the same story as the student, up to the point of the sexual touching, which he denied absolutely and vehemently. He asked if he could meet with the student, in our presence in Erica's office, to sort the matter out.

The student agreed. In this meeting, she stuck to her guns. She did not back down. She wanted to pursue the matter no further: "just get me out of his class."

That was the end of it. Erica and I talked about what happened. Normally, in cases where accounts differ, we had strong intuitive responses as to whose truth was closer to fact. Not here.
We found them equally convincing.

Before he left Old Chapel that day, the famous writer asked to speak to me in my office. He said, "If you ever meet with a female student in your office with the door closed, you're crazy. Don't do it."

Well, of course, I closed my door when I saw women students, all the time. I couldn't do my job otherwise.

But what he cautioned was thought-provoking. I did fear the consequences of a false accusation or a misinterpreted gesture, however remote the possibility. To get a reputation of making women uncomfortable would be bad news for me, as to be a dean for men only at Middlebury was certainly not what I wanted nor could afford professionally.

I was especially careful after that when I gave young women an avuncular hug, or received an appreciative one.

Students, these days especially, are big huggers. A little hug is a common form of greeting, or good-bye.

My office always opened out into a larger open reception area where other staff worked and students hung out.

That's where we hugged, with warmth and affection.

And witnesses.

Erica's Resume

Near her retirement, Erica was informed that she was being given a significant award as "Vermont Woman of the Year." She had to give a speech and was very apprehensive. The group sponsoring the award asked her to send her resume for a proper introduction at the event.

She came to me. She said, "I don't have a resume. I don't think I ever had a resume."

I had applied for a couple of other jobs in the previous few years, as a possible way to get a new start in my marriage, so we talked about what was in a resume. She knew—she had read resumes of people.

She came in the next day with her resume on a single sheet of paper with print on just half of it. She had written down her two degrees and her two positions at Middlebury (Assistant Dean of Women for one year, Dean of Students for 19).

No publications, no conference presentations, no awards. She was the Dean of Students at Middlebury—that kept her plenty busy. She was the mother of three daughters and a grandmother by the time she retired. She had horses and chickens, and a big garden and a house to maintain. She liked to cook and have people over.

That was enough. She was a woman without pretension or an iota of self-promotion.

Organization

Talking to students was my best skill, crucial to my job. I liked to talk to students. I don't talk to students as much now that I'm retired. That's obvious.

If I had any gifts in my job as dean, they were that I was intuitive and empathetic. I believed I had a sense of how students *felt*. I remembered how I felt when I was a student, how I wanted to be treated, and I responded to them from that place in me.

I was not known for my organizational and management skills, though I think I was better than my reputation (my reputation was that I couldn't organize a fire drill). I contend that there was a method to my madness, the hint of a method anyway. On the other hand, it may indeed be that I was an organizational disaster.

I was trained by Erica Wonnacott and Frank Kelley that the Dean of Students was the Dean of *Students,* not the Dean of the College Handbook, though to be sure we were the face of the Administration, the interface between students and the rules and policies of the College.

We interpreted and enforced the *Handbook.* We often told students things they didn't want to hear. But we felt we also had a broader responsibility, a concern for their health and well-being, both generally and in particular.

As Dean of Students, Erica Wonnacott was terrifically unorganized, always woefully behind in her paperwork. She saw students all day long. She paid little attention to her schedule, so it was a mess. She was late everywhere. She hated meetings. Her public speaking skills were modest at best, reflecting how much she hated speaking in public.

She was good in private, however, one-on-one. There was no one better, and she knew the difference between a mountain and a molehill, crucial for a Dean.

I maintain that she was a brilliant administrator. Why? Because the people who worked with her loved her totally, and they *did* have organizational skills. They covered for her. They anticipated her needs. They worked hard to please her. They would run through fire for her. Me included.

Perhaps the greatest honor of my time at Middlebury was being asked by Erica's family to give the eulogy at her memorial service in the Congregational Church. She died of ovarian cancer at 76 in March 2002.

I once told Tim Spears that I wanted my colleagues to "love" me too. I loved *them*. That was probably Erica's influence. I liked working on a team. Tim laughed at my sentimentality.

We had a national search for Erica's successor. I didn't want the job if the people who I worked closely with didn't support me.

Note that I didn't tell Tim I wanted *students* to love me. I understood that I should have their respect. They could like me, though, some of them anyway, that would be okay. But that wasn't always going to happen. I had to do some unpleasant things. It was inevitable some students would resent me, I knew that, especially young men who had issues with their dads.

I didn't mind if students didn't love me. I didn't expect that. But my colleagues...that was another matter.

Double Standard

When I was appointed dean of students after a national search, Milt Peterson, chairman of the Board of Trustees, Middlebury alum, father of three sons who graduated from Middlebury (a grandson, too), extraordinarily generous benefactor of the College, took me aside and gave me a little advice.

I was aware that a number of the trustees had not always been great fans of Erica Wonnacott, believing she was too liberal of second chances, even maternal. He thought discipline was lax under Erica—students could get away with anything, they felt.

Milt told me that I should be more like Elizabeth Kelley, "Ma" Kelley, the Dean of Women when he was a student. His contemporary at Middlebury, Frank Punderson, once described her as "hell on wheels." She was unafraid to separate students from school if they broke the rules.

This was a bit much for me. I said, "Milt, Ma Kelley was the Dean of WOMEN. I can't remember the last time we had a judicial hearing for a female student who misbehaved. Ninety-five percent of the discipline problems we have are with men!" Fact of life.

Ma Kelley disciplined girls for coming in late—after hours, being seen in a bar, wearing slacks in violation of the dress requirements for women. She threatened to kick them out for getting pregnant—and she did, seriously, many times.

Ma Kelley was the custodian of the double standard.

Fatality

I was sitting in my office in Old Chapel, on Sunday, the last day of Feb break, single at the time, happier there working than home. The phone rang, Campus Security, transferring a call from the Vermont State Police.

I was told by the officer on the other end that there had been an accident on Vermont Route 4 below Killington. A car had lost control on the icy road and was wiped out by a pick-up truck. The driver of the car was killed.

The Police had not been able to identify the driver. They did tell me that in the back seat of the car were Middlebury notebooks with a name in longhand on the cover. A quick look in our directory revealed that we indeed had a student with that name — and he lived in Starr Hall, right next to Old Chapel.

I walked next door and knocked on his door in Starr, expecting no answer.

A male voice said, "Come in," and I entered.

A young man was sitting at his desk. He greeted me. I explained what I knew — there had been an accident and his notebooks were in the car, and he filled me in: "My brother gave me a ride back to campus, dropped me off, and headed back to Boston."

Then he asked me, "Is he all right?"

The moment of truth. I had not prepared remarks in my head. I hesitated and choked out the words, "the crash was fatal."

The crash was fatal.

The rest of the afternoon is a blur. I know we came back to my office; he called his parents and the State Police. We went back to his room. My job was to be present and empathetic. I did my best. He was quiet, wept.

I don't remember the sad aftermath very well: someone, a relative probably, came for him and he left to be with his family.

I have no doubt that I provided the appropriate administrative follow-up and I saw him when he came back.

But what stays with me from this incident is, "the crash was fatal."

Reduced by circumstance to euphemism.

Expelled!

He put a hole in my office wall!

When I told him the verdict of the Student Judicial Council, he exploded backwards in his chair up and put *a hole in my wall* in the Dean of Students Office.

This was the father of the student who was being expelled, halfway through his senior year—"expelled" meaning never to come back and earn his degree. Banished forever. Doesn't happen very often.

Here's the story: The SUV was parked, motor running, on the sidewalk in front of the A-frames, two small dorms on the northern edge of campus.

The Campus Security officer, on walking patrol, went over to investigate why the car was on the sidewalk at night. She reached in the open driver's side window, placed her hand on the driver's shoulder, and asked him to get out of the car—whereupon he floored it, and in the process broke the officer's wrist when it was struck by the door frame.

We charged the student with "disrespect to a college official" etc. and detailed his offenses. He chose to have his case heard by the student panel.

The Council met at night. The Chief Justice came in the following morning and reported to the dean the outcome—the dean took it from there. That was the process.

I sat in my office early that morning with the director of Campus Security, who was very concerned that the student would get off with a slap on the wrist and he would have a major morale problem in his shop.

He was as surprised by the verdict of expulsion as I was.

As you might imagine, President Olin Robison's phone rang off the hook—the parents, Middlebury friends of the parents, lawyers called in outrage, par for the course, and threatened all kinds of legal repercussions.

Olin sent for me to come to his office and asked if I thought the penalty was fair. I had no history with the student or his parents. I told him I thought it was severe, out of scale.

He asked what the deans might have done. I explained that I didn't go to the hearing, but on the face of it I would have endorsed kicking him out of school, a long suspension—at least a year, with many conditions for his return.

So that's what he did—the President declared that to be the punishment, overruling the Student Judicial Council.

So the students on the Council all quit in protest, contending that there was nothing in the *Handbook* giving the President the authority to overturn their verdict.

Olin basically maintained, "I'm the President. I can do this." There were inevitable suggestions that his decision was based on money, the parents' largesse, but that wasn't the case.

He didn't throw me under the bus, didn't say he was acting on the dean of students' recommendation, and I appreciated that, but it would have been okay if he had said that.

It blew over. The deans heard judicial cases for the rest of the year. A new Council was empaneled for the following year.

A couple years later, I had a conversation with one of the former Council members and he revealed to me that the Campus Security officer had happened upon a drug transaction, and that was the basis for their draconian verdict.

Of course, none of this had been in the charge, or a part of the hearing. The students on the Council, some of them anyway, were aware of this information, but we, the deans, weren't. I don't know if it was true.

That explained their verdict, but it still didn't justify it. You can't convict someone of something he wasn't charged with.

LMPP

My advice: if you're a teacher, be good to your students—
someday you may work for them. That's what happened to me.

Tim Spears was trained at Yale and Harvard and came to work
at Middlebury in 1988 as a professor in American Studies, my
department. He has served in the Administration as the Dean of
the College, Vice President for Administration, and now Provost.
He's a certified big shot.

I was his 10th grade English teacher. I taught for six years at
University School in Cleveland, the high school Tim attended.
I used to joke, in Tim's presence, that he got a C+ in my course,
but that was unlikely indeed.

For at least ten years at Middlebury I reported directly to him.
He wrote my annual reappointment and salary letter. I had
34 one-year contracts.

When he was making the decision to come to Middlebury as a
young faculty member, we went out to dinner, the two of us,
and talked about life in Middlebury, Vermont.

He asked me at one point, "You still teaching the LMPP?"

Ah, the LMPP—"Lindholm Method for Perfect Papers," a writing
class for new students. Tim remembered it from high school.

Indeed I was.

The LMPP was a ten-step approach that I have presented
somewhat tongue-in-cheek to students in my writing classes over
time. It emphasized Revision ("revise!" was steps 6,7,8).

Step 3 was "Mull." I told students that I subscribed to a Neo-Platonic concept of writing: perfect papers existed intact in another realm and students had to be in a state of grace to call them in. You had to *think* a paper before you wrote it and you had to be in a physical space that pleased you and appealed to your Muse.

I contended that the academic rhythm with all its deadlines was the enemy to good writing. Step 10 was "Rewrite."

It was whimsical and impractical, but Tim remembered it from years before.

When I retired, years later, Tim, then the Vice President for Administration, read the "minute" at the faculty meeting that acknowledged my nearly four decades at Middlebury.

Anatomical Impossibility

I was working with a student who was having great difficulty writing his senior thesis in history. He was blocked, couldn't write. We had pretty much run out of options—extensions, incompletes, other considerations.

He would get an F on the thesis and the opportunity to submit it at a later date. The F would stand though, remain on his transcript. (As it turned out, he changed his major, and took an additional year to finish.)

I had conversed some with his dad, a captain of industry, a big-time corporate executive.

In May, near the end of school, he called me and asked if I could see him and his son on an upcoming Saturday morning. He would be traveling to Middlebury from the West Coast.

At our meeting, I was struck that, despite the fact that it was 9:00 in the morning, on a weekend, he was dressed in a three-piece suit. His son was attired in a t-shirt and overalls, no shoes. Quite a contrast.

At the outset, he said to me, "I'm here, Dean Lindholm, in the hope that the two of us can help my son get his head out of his ass."

That invitation gave me some insight into the complications of his son's life.

Fire

It seemed like the frat wars went on forever.

Treasurer Dave Ginevan, Professor Russ Leng, and I comprised a small committee that President Robison designated in 1986 to negotiate with the fraternity alumni councils for the sale of their houses to the College.

We held a series of lunches at the Middlebury Inn. Dave did most of the talking, laying out the College's offer and the rationale for their selling.

Dave was responsible for the College's fiscal health during a time of remarkable growth for the College in the 1980s and 90s. He had his own kids in college and understood the whole school, how we all worked together.

This day we were meeting at the Inn with Ted Mooney '56, President of the Sig Ep alumni board. Dave was doing most of the talking, presenting the College's position.

Dave, at that time, was a smoker. When speaking, he would take a drag from his cigarette and then cup his chin in his palm, with the cigarette between his middle and index fingers by his ear.

In the middle of his presentation to Ted Mooney, Russ interrupted, saying calmly, "Dave, your hair's on fire."

And so it was.

I would have collapsed in embarrassment. But not Dave. He patted the side of his head, put out the fire, and continued his peroration.

Dave Ginevan was another hero of mine at Middlebury College.

Dave Ginevan,
Treasurer and
Vice President for Finance

Cancer Sticks

Erica's daughter, Megan '81, told me Erica smoked a cigarette the day she died.

At staff meetings, she and Dave sat together in a smoky haze at the end of the long table in the elegant Board Room.

Dave was a tall (6'5" or so), a skinny guy. He stopped smoking and became a tall overweight guy. He died too young: I don't know if the cigarettes or the absence of cigarettes got him.

Erica never stopped. At 5:00 p.m. after her appointments, she would sit in her office and do her correspondence and light up. I often needed to talk to her at the end of the day about matters of urgent mutual concern. She was embarrassed by her smoking. She exhaled, and then took her hand and waved it above her head to disperse the smoke. It was a characteristic gesture. I will always remember it. She was so strong in so many ways, I gave her a pass on the smoking. She loved to smoke.

The Turning Point

I think Dave Ginevan undertook the decisive gesture in the protracted frat wars. It was just a short walk on campus, took less than an hour.

Commencement Day 1978 or 1979: Dave took a small group of Trustees on a tour of the fraternities early in the morning before graduation ceremonies.

The Sunday morning of Commencement is at the end of so-called Senior Week, an emotional time for students as they say good-bye to one another and this place. It is also a depressing time of extraordinary excess, or at least it was when we had frats, and I'm sure there's still has an element of that.

One of the houses on the hill, ritualistically, the night before graduation, had a big bonfire where everything that was unwanted or wouldn't fit in the car—furniture, books, whatever was combustible—was burned, and a copious amount of alcohol was consumed.

I was often on campus during Senior Week.

The Trustees who accompanied Dave were the leaders of the Board, men who had attended Middlebury, belonged to fraternities, and remembered nostalgically that time. They weren't at all sure that we were headed in the right direction in our oversight of these places that were so significant to them in their student years.

For my friends who got after me for not being more supportive of frats, I would always say, "Come to campus, visit your old house, unannounced, then come talk to me. Times change."

On that Sunday morning, Senior Week, the fraternity houses were a disaster. They were wrecked: broken furniture and windows. They stunk of stale beer, an inch of which was sticky on the floor. The Trustees were powerfully affected. It was not as they had remembered.

The Trustees as a whole, including these old frat guys, then determined that no Middlebury student should live in these deplorable spaces, regardless of who actually owned the building.

The fraternities would be renovated, rendered livable, and brought up to code. An independent contractor would determine the cost of renovations.

For four of the six houses, those costs exceeded the value of the house and their alumni boards quickly sold to the College. The two strongest houses, Chi Psi and Delta Upsilon, tried for a year to raise the funds for renovation to code, then gave up and sold. The College bought the houses at fair market value.

There would be many more comings and goings, and, yes, the outrage of the DU toga party and the bloodied mannequin which brought the College national attention in 1989, but it was the purchase of the houses, I believe, that gave the College the clear authority to intervene that it had lacked before—and in retrospect established the course of action that ended fraternities at Middlebury.

I believe that Dave Ginevan tour of the houses was the turning point, a watershed moment.

Escape

>Desperate
>running
>under a black-streaked sky
>heart pounding
>feet pounding on asphalt
>all the way
>to Peter's house
>and the promise of safety
>however fleeting.

No one home
I took his truck
keys on the floor
drove to an old chapel
a sanctuary
and the paperwork
trappings of order
and blessed calm.

At my desk
I fell asleep reassured
chaos was stayed

for now.

Khaki Pants

As my first marriage was disintegrating, and after our divorce,
I spent a lot of time at work, virtually living in my office in Old
Chapel for spells. It was a place of solace and my friends there,
my co-workers, were my support. I will forever be grateful to
them—Erica, Frank, Janet, Ann, Peggy, Arlinda, Martha, Cindy,
Deb, Karen, and others—for seeing me through this time.

My work in the Dean of Students Office required me to engage
intimately with others, students: just the distraction from my own
painful affairs that I needed, day to day.

Erica retired in the spring of 1988. The school undertook a
national search for her successor. Another finalist with me was
Ann Craig Hanson, who had been a dean at Dartmouth and was
earning her PhD from University of California. Everyone who
interviewed Ann was impressed and liked her very much.

I was pleased to be appointed Erica's successor. Ann came to the College as Associate Dean of the College and Special Assistant to the President—and we worked for three years in adjacent offices and enjoyed a close working relationship.

When Tim Light came through and shuffled the deck, Ann became the Dean of Students. She survived him, our one-year President, and served for nearly 20 years in that role.

Ann and I are friends, I'm happy to say. Her boy, Matt, and my boy, Dave, now in their 30s, are very close.

One early morning during Ann's and my time together in the Dean's Office, we were all assembled in the large outer reception area in the Dean of Students' Office in Old Chapel, just shooting the breeze before the onslaught of the day. I loved these morning rituals, starting the day with these people.

Dean's Office, 1989: l-r. Martha Mathis, Assistant Dean;
Cindy Rigg, Director of Undergraduate Records;
John Emerson, Dean of the College; Arlinda Wickland,
Associate Dean of Students; Karl Lindholm, Dean of Students;
Ann Hanson, Associate Dean of the College

Ann made fun of my attire, a style safely described as nondescript Yankee, and that's just the way I like it. Lots of tan and black and navy blue. She observed how hard it is for women, by contrast, who have to change their outfits every day.

"Look at Karl," she complained. "He's had those khaki pants on every day this week, and nobody even notices."

"Not true," I said. "I just put these on. They're fresh and clean."

"Oh, right," she said, disbelieving.

"I can prove it."

I went into my office and pulled out six pairs of nearly identical khakis out of my file cabinet. I was on my way later that day to the dry cleaners.

"Ha!"

Garbage

It was the last day of one of these one-to-two week junkets of study abroad advisers from all over the U.S. visiting universities in Britain. We were in Glasgow, Scotland, and those of us flying out the next day were having dinner in an Indian restaurant. We were relaxed; our meetings were over.

There were about a dozen or so of us, an interesting collection, diverse by age, geography, and institution. We had shared a stimulating time with representatives from these U.K. universities, and one another. We were high on the experience even before we had a drink (or two) with dinner.

*In Scotland, advisers from (l-r) Smith, Georgetown,
Redlands, Skidmore, Davidson, Dickinson,
Mt. Holyoke, Trinity (CT), and Middlebury.*

I was between marriages, describing my misadventures being single all of a sudden in my 40s, with two young kids for lengthy periods of time. Jon Ramsey of Skidmore was doing his impeccable Indian accent, and George Boyd of Trinity College in San Antonio was telling us about life in the Lone Star State.

I was especially expressive in describing my inadequacies in the kitchen, cooking. Sylvia, the dignified study abroad adviser from Wellesley, was moved to speak personally about her domestic life. She had married late (to an American academic!) and they had one daughter who was in middle school.

"I cook dinner every night," she said, "for my husband and daughter, and every night at the end of the meal, my husband says, 'Thank you, dear, for a wonderful meal.'"

I said, predictably, "Aw, that's nice."

"No, it's not," she said emphatically. "You can't believe the garbage I put before that man some nights—and always he says 'Thank you, dear, for a wonderful meal. Drives me crazy.'"

"Okay," I said speaking from experience, "but it's a lot better than what he would be eating on his own."

Diversity

The beautiful young Asian woman was standing with her parents just inside the back door of the hall in the Kirk Center. She had arrived late for this first meeting of the students in the Pre-Enrollment Program in August, 1993.

I was the director that year. I worked in the Program for 19 years, most of that time teaching the Writing class. I found few of my various tasks as Dean as satisfying.

The Pre-Enrollment Program was a three-week, early introduction to Middlebury in August for first-year students who could benefit from this support. Students took four classes: a writing class, a math class, a learning skills class, and an interdisciplinary seminar taught on the undergraduate model (lectures plus discussion groups).

They made connections with staff and faculty members who could be a source of continuing support, received effective academic advising in choosing their courses, and gained a familiarity with the place that eased what might have been a difficult transition. Wonderful program.

It went all the way back to the late 1960s when the college, in the aftermath of the assassination of Martin Luther King Jr., aggressively attempted to broaden its effort to attract so-called "minority" students.

Officials at the College knew even then that to be considered a top-notch place we had to look more like the rest of America. Not easy in Vermont, "the whitest state in the Union." We couldn't be just a comfortable place for smart, white, affluent students who liked to ski.

If I had to pick out one word that dominated the internal discourse at Middlebury in my three and a half decades in the Administration, it would be "diversity."

I had just offered some introductory welcoming remarks to the assembled 30 students and those older adults who had come with them to Middlebury. We were going around the room with the students introducing those who brought them and telling us something about themselves.

When it was the turn of Kara Delahunt, the Asian girl, she explained that she came from suburban Boston, she was here with her dad Bill '63. She then added, "I've never been in a room with so much diversity."

Kara was adopted in 1975 at the end of the Vietnam War. She was an orphan who was part of Operation Babylift. The first plane out of Saigon in this humanitarian mission, crashed, killing 140 children. *Time Magazine* called it "a ghastly symbol of the unending agony of Vietnam."

The Delahunts were distraught, believing their baby among the casualties. To their great relief, she was on the *second* plane out.

While at Middlebury, she met and fell in love with Nicolai Bobrov, a Russian boy, a stalwart on the Middlebury National Championship ice hockey teams. They married and have two children, two Russian-Vietnamese-American children.

The new America. The new Middlebury.

Kara Delahunt was one of the babies airlifted from Saigon just prior to the evacuation in April 1975. She was adopted by Bill ('63) and Katharina Delahunt *(right, with sister Kirstin)*.

Michael Jordan, on Skates

On that same day, a group of young men sat in a knot on the right side of the room. They had just met for the first time. They were hockey players. Filip Jirousek, from Czechoslovakia, went first, followed by Emil Jattne from Sweden.

Then Francois Bourbeau and Chris Farion introduced themselves. They were both hockey goalies from Canada. It drew a laugh when they revealed that they played the same position, but Chris said, "I think we can be friends."

As it turned out, they did indeed remain friends. They split time in the goal for four years, were both All-Americans, and led the Panthers to three National Championships.

Next was a handsome, tall young black man. "I'm Mark Spence," he said. "I'm from Montreal and I play hockey."

This was more than the aunt of Cynarah Alcantara from New York City could accommodate. She said, "Come on, young man. Tell us who you *really* are."

In truth, he looked more like Michael Jordan than Wayne Gretzsky. He turned to assure her. "No, honest, I really am a hockey player, from Canada."

"My Lord," she sighed, quite bewildered by this place where even the tall, black kids play ice hockey.

Mark Spence was quite a player, playing professionally for a few years after Middlebury, and then coming back to coach at Middlebury, before embarking on a career in secondary education.

"This is your *work*?"

After our divorce, Jane and David, Jody's and my children, lived with me during all their vacations, including summer.

When I was working in the Pre-Enrollment Program, I always tried to attend lunch in Proctor with the students in the Program. It was a good way to converse informally and get to know them.

My daughter Jane enjoyed coming to lunch with me. We sat at a different table of students every day so I might get to know them. Jane was 8–11 years old the years I directed the Program.

At lunch, Jane sat there and listened to the conversations between me and the young people newly arrived at Middlebury. She liked it. My other children found this kind of conversational activity with dad sheer torture. They pulled on my sleeve and begged, "Can we *leave*, please."

After lunch, Jane and I walked down the hill from Proctor to my office in Old Chapel.

"Can I ask you a question, Dad: is this what you do, for *work*?"

My job seemed easy and interesting to her. I talked to students, all different kinds of students, students from all over with interesting lives.

After she graduated from college, years later, Jane decided to talk to people for a living too. She has worked now for some time in public radio.

She has her own show on Vermont Public Radio, the "Vermont Edition." She interviews people and she's really good at it.

Jane Lindholm, host of VPR's Vermont Edition

No Clothes

It was a summer day, midday. I parked in the Arts Center lot, adjacent to the track, intending to run ten laps, two and a half miles, my normal run. I preferred the track to the roads, that surface being more forgiving. My knees were already giving me trouble. I'd eventually have them both replaced.

As I entered the track, a faculty friend was leaving. She had finished her workout. We were work-friends, having served together on a variety of projects. She was a respected scholar and teacher, and quite beautiful, a fact not lost on me or others. I was attracted to her, quite naturally, but not to the point of ever risking impropriety. I wasn't married at the time, but she was.

We chatted amiably. She allowed that she was working out in order to lose ten pounds.

I said that I thought she looked quite fit.

She said, "But you should see me with no clothes on."

She blushed.

I bit my tongue. Sign of maturity.

Hot Commodity

On occasion, when a faculty marriage fell apart, I would get a call. It was a compliment, I guess, more or less.

Evidently, I was an expert of some kind. I was held up as an example that there was life after such a break-up. I did not lobby for such a role.

I remember well a lunch at Rosie's Restaurant with such an aggrieved faculty member. He explained to me his situation: he had been a tenured professor at another fine institution, married to another scholar. He left his job and came to Middlebury when his wife was appointed to a tenure-track position here. He took on a part-time teaching role at Middlebury

She fell in love with another, after receiving tenure at Middlebury, filed for divorce and married him.

My lunch companion was angry, embittered. "How could she do this to me after what I sacrificed for her!"

I shrugged, "She doesn't like you anymore. She likes him better. No mystery. It's as old as time."

"She did you a favor," I said. "There's nothing worse than living with someone who doesn't like you."

He felt diminished, broken by this experience. He thought it would be difficult to meet someone else. "I feel like I'm 'damaged goods,'" he said.

I disagreed. I gave him the demographic argument. "You're a man in his 40s with a job and a skill and a future and no visible defects. Relax. Look at the numbers—women are going to call *you*. You're not 'damaged goods,' you're a 'hot commodity.'"

That wasn't far from the truth, no mere pep talk. When I saw him on campus in subsequent months, he would give me a wink and a thumbs-up, and say, "hot commodity."

After a few years, he too remarried, had a child, and still greets me with a smile.

Don't Jump!

I liked talking to the *Campus* when I was a Dean, even though I knew they were trying to stick it to me as a member of the dreaded Administration. The *Campus* sees itself in an adversarial role, as the voice of student opinion, a necessary counter-balance to the unchecked power of Old Chapel.

I tried to put the best face on what the College was doing. But I also identified with *Campus* reporters and editors from my years as a student on the paper. They were trying to get a story.

I was amused that the Administration was constantly referred to as a building, "Old Chapel," like the White House or the Pentagon. I would often ask who in Old Chapel is responsible for the latest outrage—the President, the Dean of the College, the Treasurer, me? I pictured Old Chapel cartoonishly as a malevolent pulsating form.

I always worried, with reason, that I talked too much to the *Campus*. Often a 30-minute conversation was distilled to a few quotations that conformed to a point of view of the interviewer.

I was seldom misquoted, but often quoted *out of context*, (as those who talk too much frequently complain). When that happened, the key question was always—do I write a clarifying follow-up letter to the *Campus*, or not? To do so was usually my impulse. It cleared the air and allowed for a more accurate presentation of the issue.

But it also served to maintain the matter in the public discourse. Time passes quickly in the school year. The *Campus* was, and remains, a weekly, publishing only 20 or so issues a year. Often we're better off just letting it go.

One time I was misquoted and had no choice but to follow up.

For a time, before we had a safety officer, I was in charge of fire safety. I worked closely with Jon Woodbury, a colleague in Buildings and Grounds whom I greatly admired. Shortly after a terrible fire at Providence College in which eight students died, I gave a basic fire safety talk in Dana Auditorium.

One of the fundamental messages was that people most often die in fires from smoke inhalation, not from immolation. The fire at Providence was in a dorm configured much like our Gifford Hall. A number of students leapt to their death from their dorm windows. They would have survived if they had stayed in their rooms.

I told students to close their doors in a fire, stay in their rooms if there's smoke in the hall, plug the narrow opening under the door with damp towels, and wait for help.

Stay put!

The subsequent *Campus* article had one small mistake. It omitted the word "not" or "never" and wrote the following statement: "Dean Lindholm emphasized that students should jump out of their windows in a dorm fire."

I did write that time with a correction.

Brigitte Bardot

I was sitting at my desk in the Dean of Students Office in Old Chapel at the end of the day, after everyone else had left. This was a common situation in the years between marriages when I virtually lived in my office. The phone rang and I answered it.

That was my first mistake.
An Associated Press reporter was on the line. He told me he had a few questions about Winter Term at Middlebury. Specifically, he had some questions about a particular course.

I knew what he was after. I told him, "You really don't want to talk to me. You should talk to someone on the Curriculum

Committee. They oversee Winter Term. Here I'll give you the number of its chairman, Robert Gleason."

"I have a deadline," he said, "I need this tonight. Let me just ask you a few questions."

"I really don't know much about Winter Term classes. I just work in the Dean of Students Office." He persisted. I relented.

"So this class," he said, "is about Brigitte Bardot."

"Right."

"And the students watch her movies for the class?"

"Of course."

He paused.

This was before "popular culture" had achieved some respectability in the curriculum. A class on Brigitte Bardot was news, but defensible.

Then he asked, "How many students are in the class?"

"A lot," I said.

"Over a hundred?" He knew how many were in the class.

"Yes."

"Most of the football team?"

"Some football players are in the class, yes."

"Listen," I added, making my second and fatal mistake. "This is a real class. It's called the Cult of Personality," and I added a few other *bon mots*.

"Thank you, Dean Lindholm."

The teacher of the class was a young female professor of French who thought the class would be of limited appeal, so she put no limit on the course size. When registration was announced, she saw that 175 students had signed up. You can bet the next year the Curriculum Committee had size limits on all classes.

Jonathan Yardley wrote a column in the *Washington Post* decrying the absence of rigor and seriousness of purpose in higher education, using our Bardot course as exhibit A. The *Boston Globe* ran a feature story under the headline: "Brigitte Bardot: A Lesson in What Lures Students to Class."

The *Globe* piece took this paragraph, right off the AP wire:

"Middlebury's associate dean of students, Karl Lindholm, agreed: 'It is a very legitimate winter term course. It is easy to parody its content, a bunch of post-adolescents watching dirty movies but it has intellectual content. The mistake we made is that we should have had limited enrollment. This is the biggest number of students I can remember in a course, at least this year.'"

The next day, I started receiving phone calls from friends far and wide who had seen my name in print. Hundreds of newspapers nationwide quoted "Karl Lindholm," defending this class, in sections called "People in the News" or some such.

I got dozens of clippings, one from a former student living in Alaska. I still have them. My favorite is a clipping with small pictures of Brigitte Bardot and Paul Newman and underneath them my name in bold type making that pithy comment.

Even today, if you Google "Brigitte Bardot" "Karl Lindholm" you get three hits, from newspapers in Washington D.C., Michigan, and Los Angeles.

Me and BB—pretty good company.

Maxim

The best advice I got for being a Dean came second-hand from Brett's mother who told her to remember always that "the thing you're worried about is not the thing that's gonna get you."

Nothing in Dean's work could be more true.

There were always five things on my desk, or in my head, to do that could blow up at any time and be a mess. But he worst messes came out of the blue, entirely unanticipated.

So the moral of the story is you might as well relax and take things as they come.

Not that easy.

A Father's Shame

It was summer, finally. I was sitting at my desk, with some welcome uninterrupted time to work on long put-off projects— cleaning up after the school year.

A square-jawed man appeared in my doorway, unannounced. He greeted me as "Dean Lindholm," and told me, "My daughter was raped in one of your dorms this spring."

That got my attention. It wasn't how I expected to start my day. I invited him to sit down at the table and tell me what he knew. Turns out his daughter had visited one of our first-year dorms in the spring in the company of a high school friend. His daughter had been served alcohol, then had sex with one of our students.

The student was 18. His daughter was 15. The sex thus constituted "statutory rape."

I consulted with the local authorities and asked them if they would pursue a rape case against an 18-year-old boy and a 15-year-old girl when both parties concurred the sex had been consensual, and they said they probably would not.

But still we had a mess.

Subsequent conversations with the father, a couple of times at Rosie's Restaurant, convinced me that his was a human response: he was afraid he was losing his daughter—and as a moral exemplar in the community, he was humiliated by her behavior. All he wanted was an apology and a chance to meet with the boy.

I reported this to the boy's parents. His father, a lawyer, was concerned about the ramifications an admission would entail. Nonetheless, we set up a meeting with both families.

At this meeting, the boy said, "I like your daughter, sir. We saw each other after that night. I didn't know she was 15. I'm sorry." His sincerity was obvious, and genuine.

When the girl's father, a minister, suggested he would like to engage the boy in moral instruction, the other father quickly but respectfully demurred, "We're Roman Catholics. We go to church every Sunday. We'll handle that."

The families embraced as they left the office. That part was over. We did pursue judicial charges against another young man who had provided the alcohol to these underage students. His parents were unhappy with me and made angry calls to the Dean of the College and the President.

I don't know if I did the right thing or not. As Dean of Students I had wide latitude in those days. I tried to do what I felt was right.

In my last Middlebury assignment as Dean of one of our residential commons from 2008–2010, I would have responded to this situation very differently. I would have taken the essential information from the father, thanked him very much, and reported the incident to the HMO, Human Relations Officer. She would have taken it from there.

Spaceman

I taught my first baseball class at Middlebury in 1986. If you live long enough, what's out becomes in. My interest is popular culture, baseball, and my approach interdisciplinary.

These days, *mirabli dictu*, popular culture is legitimate and the interdisciplinary approach is where it's at (cf. Environmental Studies, International Studies, Neuroscience).

My keenest interest in baseball is during the era of segregation in America, from Plessy vs Ferguson (1896) to Brown vs Board of Education, Topeka, KS (1954). What a fascinating period in American history.

In the depths of the Great Depression, the black baseball experience thrived, reflecting a vigorous subterranean culture. One scholar referred to the Negro leagues baseball's "Atlantis," a lost world.

My heroes are the men who climbed in their cars with tape recorders in the 1970s and interviewed all the great Negro league players.

They knew that statistical comparisons between the white and black players were unreliable, because of the variability of competition and inconsistencies in the written record in black baseball, so they asked these players born too soon, "Tell me what it was like."

And they told stories, wonderful stories, of life in the baseball world, so important to the black community and so distant from mainstream (white) America's baseball absorption.

The greatness of these players and teams would be preserved and conveyed orally, fittingly enough, like so much in the African-American historical record.

Eventually I taught two baseball courses in the American Studies program—a general course called "Baseball, Literature, and American Culture," and a more narrowly focused course, "Segregation in America: Baseball's Negro Leagues."

Enter the Spaceman.

Over the years, Bill "Spaceman" Lee became my "closer," serving as the guest lecturer in the last class in my baseball courses.

Now it's a tradition.

He has lived in Craftsbury, Vermont, for the past 30 years, having bought a hillside plot from a Vermonter he met one

Spaceman holding forth on the last day of "Segregation in America: Baseball's Negro Leagues, Spring Term 2015

winter at a Red Sox fantasy camp. He built a lovely, modest home there. It is his base of operations.

Bill Lee was a hero of many of us in the 1960s. He was an oxymoron: a counterculture baseball player. Make no mistake — he could play. He was an ace on a National Championship baseball team at the University of Southern California and won 116 games for the Red Sox in the Major Leagues. He's in the Red Sox Hall of Fame.

He was suspended briefly and fined by Commissioner Bowie Kuhn for admitting he used marijuana. He won an appeal of his fine, saying he "used" marijuana, but didn't "smoke" it: he put it on his cereal.

The students in the class are blown away when he presides, as they are accustomed to former athletes offering the usual bromides ("work hard," "sacrifice," "live clean," "get ahead"). Bill just riffs on whatever questions they ask him, and what happens to be on his mind.

I remember early in our relationship some fifteen years ago I was trying to reach him about my class. I called his home in Craftsbury and got this recorded message: "It's Sunday night," I was calling on *Thursday*, "and I'm headed north. When hunting ducks you gotta lead 'em. If you want me, you better lead me by about . . . Saskatoon."

We eventually connected. He was in Vancouver, in the middle of a five-week barnstorming tour of western Canada with other former major league ballplayers. That night, they had beaten the Vancouver Police Department in a nailbiter, 16–14.

What I love about Bill Lee is that he doesn't trade on his past. He just loves baseball and playing baseball. He plays all the time. He goes to the fantasy camps of the Red Sox and Montreal Expos and plays in different tournaments in Florida and Arizona in the months when baseball can't be played in Vermont.

He talks to students about what he's doing *now*—which is, still, playing baseball. He'd rather talk about a Vermont senior league game between the Burlington Cardinals, his team, and another group of hoary Vermonters, than pitching in the seventh game of the World Series in Fenway (which he did in 1975—and left the game with a 3–2 lead in the seventh inning).

In summer 2016, the Cardinals won the Vermont Senior League Championship defeating, over the course of three Sundays, the Middlebury Woodchucks 2–1 in 11 innings, then knocking off the top-seeded Colchester Cubs in another pitcher's duel, 3–1, and winning it all in 12 innings against the Montpelier Monties.

Bill pitched every inning of every game (his catcher for the Cardinals is Miro Weinberger, the mayor of Burlington, who played at Yale).

The Vermont Senior League is an over-35 league. Bill is *69 years old*, the oldest player in the league.

Paternity (Vietnam)

Some classes are better than others. By "classes," I don't mean "courses," though some courses are better than others, to be sure. Some individual classes are memorable indeed.

My Vietnam War course was called "Telling a True War Story: Vietnam," after Tim O'Brien's *The Things They Carried*.

I don't think I'll teach that course again: too hard to go back in time and experience those feelings again.

For me, the course didn't lend itself to objective, dispassionate analysis. That's why I'm glad it was a literature course—we could embrace the subjective experience of young Americans (me!) then.

The Vietnam course had many visitors. I asked my Middlebury friends who had served there to come and talk to students. Jon

Coffin riveted them with his intensity. John Morton '68 talked about being in the Army, feeling safe, training in Alaska for the Olympic biathlon, the shock of getting orders for Vietnam, and spending a year in the Mekong Delta as a liaison officer.

John Morton

Jaye Roseborough, Director of Career Services for many years, came from a military family and shared her experience for a year in the USO in Vietnam as a "Donut Dolly."

Professor of Art Eric Nelson talked about being drafted out of college, going to Vietnam as a tank gunner, and ending up instead drawing propaganda leaflets, such as this one:

bạn có biết
BAO GIỜ
được trở về
với gia đình không?
Có thể là KHÔNG, vì bọn
cán bộ đã muốn các bạn
chấp nhận "SINH BẮC
TỪ NAM"

The most memorable class in the half dozen or so times that I taught the Vietnam course was in 1993 when three Middlebury students born in Vietnam came to class and told their stories.

Hieu Nguyen '92 was working at the time as assistant director of residential life at Middlebury. He later left that role for a position in our development office, and then moved on to Bates and Bowdoin. Now, he is the associate vice chancellor for development at the University of California-Riverside.

He described the "craziness" of his departure from Vietnam with his mother and grandmother from their home in Dalat, a former French resort city 75 miles northwest of Saigon. They were evacuated from Saigon on April 27, 1975, just two days before the Communists swept into the city, spent a month in a refugee camp in Guam, and then another two months at Fort Chafee, Oklahoma, before heading to Glastonbury, Connecticut, where they were sponsored by the Congregational Church.

Hieu gravitated early to sports and that interest took him to the Loomis-Chafee School in Hartford. He earned an appointment to West Point, which he entered in the fall of 1988. He realized "something was missing" for him and transferred to Middlebury, where he thrived. He earned All-American honors as a lacrosse goalie.

In the course of his presentation, Hieu said, "I don't know who my father is. I think he was a French or American soldier."

In the question-and-answer period, one of the students delicately pursued the issue of his father and what his mother told him about his identity.

"I haven't asked her about my father," he said. "If she wants me to know, she will tell me."

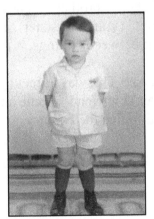

Hieu Nguyen '92

Long Lost Brother

Germaine Trong '94 is our most recent Rhodes Scholar, spending the year after she graduated from Middlebury at Oxford. She was also in class that day and told us about finding a brother she didn't even know existed.

She too left Vietnam as a small child in the chaos of the evacuation in April, 1975. Her family had literally ten minutes to pack up and leave.

At Middlebury, she decided to study abroad in her junior year. The School for International Training (SIT) had a program in Vietnam, and she told the class about her experience.

She was hoping to be a student, just doing research and going to class. Early on, she visited an aunt and was greeted by a young man, who despite his youth appeared to Germaine as if he had lived a hard life with rough dark skin and blackened teeth.

She greeted him with "Chao anh" (hello, brother), a customary greeting. He addressed her as "emut" (youngest sister), a familial title, a term of endearment between siblings.

She came to realize that this man, Anh Thi, was in fact her older brother who had been sleeping over at a friend's home and left behind on the night her family had to flee the country.

Germaine Trong

Pirates

The third student in that class, Binh Vo '96, didn't leave
Vietnam during the mayhem of the evacuation. His family didn't
have American friends. They escaped the repression after the
"American war" as "boat people" four years later.

Their journey was an odyssey of danger and desperation. His
family and others left Vietnam in a frail boat under the cover
of a tropical storm. As they were stealthily boarding, a father
slipped and dropped a baby girl, who was not recovered.

They were fired on by soldiers as they left, but not chased because of the storm. They drifted for days at sea, finally being spotted by an American helicopter and picked up by a Norwegian ship.

Binh Vo and his grandmother in Vietnam

"We were lucky not to be attacked by pirates," Binh told the class.

They were taken to Singapore where they remained in a refugee camp for three months, before coming to Denver in December of 1979, where they had sponsors.

Binh too, studied in his junior year with the SIT program in Vietnam. He was there for the 20th year celebration of the "liberation of the South"—and for the normalization of relations with the United States. He was surprised at how comfortable he was in Ho Chi Minh City (Saigon).

Binh was a delightful young man, open and artless. I still have the postcards he sent to me from Vietnam during his year abroad.

Soon after graduation he left the family home in Denver and returned to Vietnam, where he put his bicultural awareness to good use in business, eventually building up "a series of relocation companies that specialized in helping government officials and corporate transplants get settled in Vietnam."

Recently, I was shocked and saddened to read that Binh's life had taken a most dramatic turn: he is currently serving an eight-year prison sentence for his central role in a visa scam with a corrupt American Embassy official.

Drinking in English

One of the years I was on President's Staff, John Berninghausen of the Chinese Department was the acting vice president of the Language Schools, as Ed Knox was in Paris on sabbatical.

In the spring, John was talking about his intention to really enforce the Language Pledge in the summer. No English would be spoken on his watch, upon threat of dismissal from the school. Heads would roll.

"Quite frankly," he said, "the problem is with our undergraduates in the summer schools. They have late-night parties and seem only to be able to drink in English."

That cracked me up: our students can only drink in English.

Half a Million Bucks

Olin Robison told this story one day at a staff meeting with obvious delight:

His secretary, Marles, received a call one morning from Dave LaRose in the mailroom. Dave had opened a letter that was addressed simply to "Middlebury College, Middlebury VT." No return address, no designated recipient.

Dave explained that inside the letter was a check, a check for $500,000. He thought it was probably a joke, but figured he'd call the president's office first to see what they suggested he do.

Marles asked, "Who signed the check?" Dave provided the name, whereupon Marles instructed him to bring the check over to the president's office. Walk it over. Hand-carry it. Now.

The check had been written by an eccentric and powerful (and rich) member of the board, an alumnus. Good thing Dave hadn't thrown it away.

Funny story and Olin told it well.

When we got on with our business, I discreetly took out my checkbook, and wrote out and signed a check for $500,001 from my National Bank of Middlebury account, not to be outdone by a fellow alum. I handed it to Dave Ginevan, seated next to me. He looked it, and smiled and put it in his shirt pocket.

Between marriages, I was living pretty much from paycheck to paycheck. I had no savings and my checking account was usually a little short at the end of each month. I had no money.

The next week at staff meeting, when it was Dave's turn to talk, he took out my check and held it up. "This is how fundraising works," he said. "The word got out about the half-million-dollar gift and the way it was presented to us. Another alumnus heard about it, and decided not to be outdone, and has written us a check for 500,000 *and one* dollars."

All ten or so of the assembled college leaders at President's Staff responded warmly to this tale of friendly competition. Finally, Olin asked, "Well, Dave, who was it?"

"Why, it's Karl here."

Everyone groaned.

The Heart is a Lonely Hunter

Brett Millier was a rookie teacher in 1986. She had come to Vermont from California after finishing her PhD in English at Stanford. She drove her truck cross-country and arrived in August in time to get settled and prepare for classes.

Frank Kelley, residential life director, ran into her on campus on her first day and struck up a conversation. He was enthused to discover she taught American Literature. He asked if she would like to lead a discussion group at Bread Loaf during Freshman Orientation on Carson McCullers' *The Heart is a Lonely Hunter*, the freshman reading.

Brett thought that was a good idea, a way for a new teacher to meet new students, so Frank brought her to Old Chapel to sign her up in the dean's office.

I was organizing the program, so Frank introduced her to me, indicating her interest in leading a discussion.

So I said, with mock exasperation, "Frank, why in the world would we want an American literature professor to lead a discussion on this classic text in American literature?"

Brett's face fell. Frank led her out of the office. "Don't pay any attention to him. Trust me, he's very grateful you will participate.

"He's from Maine," he explained. "He can't help it."

The Tomayta in the Press Box

Brett has perhaps the best sports credential of anyone on the academic faculty at Middlebury.

At Yale, she had various jobs in the athletic department. The summer after she graduated, she had a Time-Life internship at *Sports Illustrated*. She then went back to Yale to work in the sports information office.

In the middle of the year, the sports information director left to take another job, so Brett became the SID.

She set up the meeting of Roger Angell, the *New Yorker's* great baseball writer, and 92-year-old Smokey Joe Wood, the great Red Sox pitcher (34–5 for the 1912 World Champion Red Sox) and longtime Yale coach (20 years), when future major-league stars Frank Viola of St. John's hooked up with Yale's Ron Darling on May 21, 1981.

The brain behind the scoreboard

By Carla Marinucci
OF THE EXAMINER STAFF

SHE'S ALWAYS loved writing. But she never imagined her prose would light up the sky in letters 5-feet high.

She never dreamed every syllable would fill a stadium of thousands with thrills and tears.

She never realized how fickle is her audience. They'll shower her works with catcalls and derisive hoots in one minute; in the next, there are ecstatic ovations.

Brett Millier, her regular readers will admit, has a certain characteristic economy of expression, a *joie de vivre* in her famous prose.

"Nice catch!"

"Go, Giants!"

And her most famous line — the one that inevitably brings them to their feet — "Charge!"

If you're heading out to Candlestick Park for the Giants' opening home game today, you will read the writings of Millier, a raving maniac of a baseball fan who will earn her Ph.D in American and English literature at Stanford University this June.

Millier, 28, works Candlestick's computerized scoreboard at every home Giants game, transforming its 22,000, 40-watt blinking bulbs into an electronic cheering section — even when, as happens at Candlestick, there isn't much to cheer about.

She's responsible for the myriad of baseball statistics, the greetings and "happy birthdays" that fans request for their friends and family, the "Giants welcome ..." for the fraternities and companies, the cheers and the little trivia quizzes that flash up there and drive baseball fans mad.

"We have the only Ph.D operator in the major leagues," says a proud Tom Fielsie, who maintains the huge scoreboard for the Giants. "She's the only one who could ever remember the last thing she did when there's a problem."

Watching Millier work the huge "dinosaur" of a board — it's 14-years-old, a senior citizen in the world of major league scoreboards — is a study in quick wits, control and grace under pressure.

She sits in front of a small computerized terminal, which takes hours to program before the game, waiting for her chance to make people happy with greetings, or give them a dose of reality when it comes to the score.

There's no room for errors, which are unmercifully broadcast to the waiting crowds in lights.

"Every mistake goes right out there," she says. A previous scoreboard operator misspelled the word "deaf," and the board read: "The Giants Welcome the California School for the Death."

There was the time, suitable in its sarcasm, when an opposing infielder dropped a pop fly, and Millier hit the "Nice Catch!" button by mistake.

Nevertheless, it's a job any red-blooded American would dream about: perched up there in the press box, the smell of hot dogs wafting in, the stale cigar smoke and the nasty language of veteran sports writers drifting around, and the boos of the crowd resounding across the stadium.

"The thing I remember about this job is the beginning was freezing to death, and starving to death," Millier says.

—Please see MILLIER E-8

Brett Millier — she computes the score for the Giants at Candlestick   — Examiner/Paul Kitagaki Jr.

The outcome was a classic pitchers' duel (Darling didn't give up a hit for 11 innings, but Viola won, 1–0) and a wonderful Angell story in the *New Yorker* ("The Web of the Game").

She thought about making sports information her career, but decided instead to go to Stanford and earn a PhD in English. Her graduate school job was operating the scoreboard at Candlestick Park for the San Francisco Giants. In three seasons she saw over 240 games. Her predecessor was fired—he couldn't spell. The *coup de grace* was when he welcomed "the San Francisco School of the Death."

The TV announcer for the Atlanta Braves, John Sterling (now the Yankees announcer much despised by Red Sox fans) called her "the tomayta in the press box." She was the only woman, and got written up in the *San Francisco Examiner* and *Sporting News*.

The Giants weren't very good, and Candlestick could be a nightmare ("The coldest winter I ever spent was a summer in San Francisco," Mark Twain), but still . . .

Her keen interest in sports was okay with me.

Me and the Cops

For a couple of years, I was the associate dean of the College with a special relationship to the departments of athletics and to campus security (now called Public Safety).

Relations between the town police and security were especially dysfunctional after L'Affair Zaccaro. I was called upon to meet frequently with Chief Al Watson and his staff in the town offices, and along the way I made it a point to get to know the police officers in the town.

One day, early in our relationship, Brett and I were driving somewhere, perhaps out to get apples at Stan Pratt's orchard or to visit Peter's and Marg's sheep farm on Munger Street, or to visit her friend Abby Zito at her house on Quarry Road.

I took a right turn at the five corners past the Middlebury Inn and Grand Union and headed out Quarry Road, paying no attention to the 25 mph speed limit, driving what seemed to me a safe speed.

I saw the blue lights behind me and pulled over.

As Officer Michael Bolduc began to inquire why I was driving at a speed well above the speed limit, he recognized me and said, "Oh hi, Karl. Listen, slow down next time when you make the turn onto Quarry Road."

"Thanks, Mike."

Brett realized then she was spending time with someone with real clout in Middlebury.

Consolidation

In 1994–95, a committee led by Professor Timi Meyer met extensively to consider the best way to do study abroad. It was decided (passive voice!) that we would consolidate Middlebury and non-Middlebury study abroad in one operation under the leadership of History Professor David Macey.

Study abroad students had expanded until about 60 percent of our students were on non-Middlebury programs. Then and now, over half of the junior class was abroad for a semester or year.

I endorsed this decision 100 percent. I had been doing study abroad for a long time without portfolio—a monolinguist with a degree in American Studies. Times had changed. The world had gotten bigger, bigger than Europe. It was time.

Alas, no more study abroad trips for me. I developed my keenest professional relationship on these trips with colleagues from other schools over the country. I still have a lively email correspondence with six of those colleagues, retired now like me. We call ourselves "the Wombats," after our adventures on a couple of junkets to the Pacific Rim.

In 1995–96, Brett and I were both on sabbatical in Ogunquit, Maine, a wonderful year. Macey called me all the time. In twenty years, I had learned some stuff and he picked my brains.

I was not annoyed. I was grateful.

Overdose

Her friends insisted it was not a "serious" attempt at ending her life, just a gesture of desperation, a cry for help.

But we sent her home anyway. We're not a hospital — we're a school. This cry for help needed to be dealt with elsewhere. That was our policy.

This decision did not sit well with her friends, who loved her. The decision to send a student home is an administrative decision, based of course on the information provided by the professionals. Implementation of the decision is the often quite complicated responsibility of the Dean.

This troubled student's friends were furious with us. They asked if they could meet with me, three 18–19 year-old women, powerfully concerned about their friend and her welfare. We met with the RA in his room in Stewart Hall, a first-year dorm.

They were determined: don't send our dear friend home. That would be inhumane. That would be sending her back into the situation that created her desperation, back into the dysfunction responsible for her distress.

I was not there to negotiate. The decision had been made. I was not in a position to present alternatives. I was there to be respectful of their feelings, to listen, and not to relent.

Middlebury was her new home, they explained to me. Her new friends at Middlebury, that is to say, them, were her real family, capable of the love and support her family at home had in their view failed to provide.

I'm not sure the troubled student came back to Middlebury. I can't recall. What I remember is sitting there with those three earnest young women who loved their friend and wanted to take care of her. I doubt they ever forgave me.

Doing my job.

Not So Bad

An old friend, Kevin Hughes, a colleague from my first teaching job out of college (at Kents Hill School in Maine) was coming through Middlebury with his son, a junior in high school. We decided to meet for dinner at Mister Ups.

Kevin and his wife Marg had been important to me in those lonely first years teaching. They were only a couple years older and had started their family. They were kind to include me in their lives and I have always been grateful.

Kevin graduated from Dartmouth just a few years before me at Middlebury. Like many Dartmouth guys, Kevin did not suffer from a lack of confidence.

He and his boy were already at Mister Ups when I arrived. After opening pleasantries, Kevin said to me, "Well, you've got a friend in the bartender."

I checked the bar and saw that Sean Ferguson was tending bar. Sean was a recent Middlebury graduate, whom I knew because he had helped us in the dorms as a residence hall adviser. He was a funny guy, personable in the extreme.

Kevin had approached Sean at the bar and explained that he was meeting an old colleague he hadn't seen in a great while, "Karl Lindholm," and wondered if he knew him.

Sean said, "Yeah, I know him."

So Kevin said, "I remember him as kind of a jerk, full of himself. Is he still like that?"

"Nah, he's not a bad guy," Sean said.

"You can tell me the truth," Kevin persisted.

"No, he's okay."

"If you insist," Kevin said with apparent resignation.

Sean Ferguson is my Facebook friend now, though we haven't seen one another for years. Thanks, man. I owe you one.

Old Stone School

I think anybody who is anybody at Middlebury should be required as *a condition of employment* to visit Alexander Twilight's school and home and church in Brownington Historical village in the Northeast Kingdom of Vermont, right up near the Canadian border.

We make so much of Alexander Twilight as the first black college graduate (1823) that it constitutes hypocrisy, it seems to me, that so few take the time to go to Brownington.

The problem is the distance, I guess, about two and a half hours away. It's both far and not very far.

After Twilight graduated from Middlebury, he earned his divinity degree and settled in Brownington as the pastor and schoolmaster there. In 1834–36 he built a magnificent four-story stone (granite) schoolhouse, across from his dwelling, and down the road just 100 yards or so from his church.

The building looks remarkably like Painter Hall, where Twilight dwelt when he was a Middlebury student. No one knows exactly how Twilight was able to pull off the construction of such formidable structure in the 1830s, and myths abound.

I don't know when I first went there, probably the first time I taught a seminar called "Roads Less Traveled: Literature and Culture of Northern New England," an examination of the Yankee archetype, to which I happily identify.

The first book we read in that class is Howard Frank Mosher's *Stranger in the Kingdom*, a novel about black minister's mistreatment in Vermont's Northeast Kingdom, derived from an actual incident in the 1960s.

That black minister is the "stranger" in the title, but there's another black minister from 1800s who has an important role in the novel who is clearly patterned after Alexander Twilight, another stranger in the Kingdom.

The first weekend of that class, we all climbed into a 15-passenger van and drove to Brownington. There we were given a guided tour of the buildings and grounds along with a discussion of the history of Twilight's life in Vermont's Northeast Kingdom (an ironic term coined by Vermont Senator George Aiken for the three northernmost counties in Vermont).

On the way up, we stopped at Mosher's house in Irasburg and students met the author of the book they were reading, always a thrill.

I was astonished when I first saw Twilight's village. If you appreciate rural New England landscapes, you will find few as striking as that surrounding Brownington. The village itself is up a hill just two miles from town of Orleans. Next to Twilight's church is a field with another small hill, at the top of which is a fire tower.

At the top of that tower, you have a magnificent 360-degree view: nearby Lake Memphremagog and Canada in one direction; beautiful Lake Willoughby in another; Mount Mansfield and ripples of mountains, the Greens and the Whites, to southeast; and the Adirondacks to the west.

It is a Yankee Shangri-La, a mystical place of great beauty.

The Old Stone School

Safe Sex

The Frisbee Dog sculpture next to Munroe Hall is anatomically precise.

For a while, some art or dog lover wanted to make sure there was no proliferation of Frisbee Dogs, and so placed a condom on the dog in the appropriate place, every night.

Frank Kelley was always the first of us to arrive in the mornings. Like the farmer that he was, he awoke and got moving at the crack of dawn. After doing paperwork in his tiny office in Battell South, he would spend the rest of the day walking the campus, conducting his business first-hand, hands-on, face to face. A wonderful man, Frank was our first director of residential life. He had worked for 25 years at Middlebury High School, teaching Latin and then serving as principal. He had a farm and sixty acres in Cornwall. He and his wife Ann raised five kids.

As a colleague, he was a joy to work with. This was his last job and he spent ten years in the role (1985–95). He just wanted to help make things work. Students loved him, colleagues too.

One of his first tasks in the early morning was to decondomize the Frisbee Dog.

One morning in the fall, 1990, he ran into Timothy Light, our one-year President, on the path. The President made some request or other, so Frank fished in his pocket for a pen to write a note to himself. The contents of his pocket spilled to the ground, including the condom.

"Oh that," Frank explained to the President, picking up the condom, "I just took it off the dog."

Tim Light found us a very strange crowd.

Frank Kelley

Welcome (Russian)

Frank Kelley could do anything. I am so grateful my life included Frank. He was a Renaissance Man, but one who never drew attention to himself. He just liked to help make things *work*. He was an inspiration.

Frank wore his humility like an old barn coat. I remember speaking with him about a candidate for a job in the dean's office. There was one person he particularly favored, so he advised me, "Keep in mind, Karl, I'm a very good judge of character: I'm right about 50 percent of the time."

When his oldest son Tim decided to major in Russian at Dartmouth, Frank took beginning Russian at Middlebury summer school so he could communicate with his boy.

Frank's language training paid dividends for us at the College when President Robison took advantage of *Glasnost* and put together a large-scale educational exchange program for Russian students. About 60–100 Russian students came to our campus for a week-long Orientation in August before being dispersed to other campuses across the country.

We kept four or five of these students at Middlebury for the year. Frank made a special effort to ease their challenging transition. This small, unprepossessing man, with ubiquitous clipboard and yellow legal pad, would greet them in his rudimentary Russian.

From then on, they knew they had a friend here at Middlebury.

One spring, Frank and I took two of the Russian students to lunch at Mister Ups. We inquired about their year and asked them what impressions they had of American students, Middlebury students.

The first said, "They eat in class." The disrespect of that behavior astonished him.

The second observed, "They think 'how are you' is a greeting."

Homage

I missed him so when he retired in 1995. I suggested that we meet at Steve's Park Diner on Tuesday mornings for breakfast.

It wasn't long before others joined us—Jan Leggett, Ann Hanson, Matt Longman, and John Emerson were regulars. Others joined as well—Anya Puri, Kathy Foley. We combined two tables just inside the door.

Erica Wonnacott was slow to join us. When I encouraged her, she said, "I don't want to go and talk about the College."

"We don't talk about the College," I assured her.

She came once, and then came every week. She was so bright and vibrant. Those Tuesday mornings were as good as it gets.

September 11, 2001, happened on a Tuesday.

Frank and I were the last to leave Steve's that day. An elderly woman, whose English was very limited, French-Canadian probably, tried to tell us about the plane striking the World Trade Center. She gesticulated wildly. We were polite.
Frank and I said our good-byes and I climbed in my car and heard on the radio the scale of the evolving crisis. I didn't go to work. I went home and turned on the TV and watched live, with the rest of America, the horrifying events of the morning.

Erica contracted ovarian cancer and died in 2002, followed by Frank of congestive heart failure in 2006, and our numbers at Steve's inevitably dwindled.

Now, a few years later, I often go there on Tuesdays, by myself. I bring a project to work on or something to read. Sometimes I run into people there I know and drink coffee with them.

I feel I am in Frank's and Erica's presence.

Frosh Orientation

I love Bread Loaf. When people ask me the difference between Middlebury and other liberal arts small colleges in the northeast, I say "How many have a campus in the mountains?"

I once mentioned to Frank that my dream was to run Frosh Orientation at Bread Loaf. He said, "Let's do it."

And we did!

Frank was a master logician. He made all the practical arrangements—the school buses to get kids up there, the vans to get them to their hikes in the mountains, the arrangements for the overnight at Bread Loaf, dining hall arrangements, everything.

So we divided the class in half and ran an academic orientation on campus for one group and a stimulating day in the Green Mountains at Bread Loaf for another. The next day we switched.

The Bread Loaf Orientation included a morning panel with faculty discussing the assigned Frosh reading, followed by small group discussions.

Then in the afternoon we sent everyone out into the woods. There were long hikes and short hikes—and even no hikes. For new students who didn't want to hike, Gary Margolis walked them to the Robert Frost cabin and introduced them to the bard of Ripton. A biology professor took others into the woods surrounding Bread Loaf and identified the flora and fauna of the immediate region. Something for everyone.

It was chaos in the theater as I sent the students off in their prearranged groups. Then, boom, all of a sudden, it was quiet: 250 kids out in the Green Mountains.

A young intern in our counseling office approached me and said breathlessly, "What a great job you have!"

"Are you kidding?" I said. "I just sent 250 kids out into the woods. I don't know who has diabetes and forgot their insulin, I don't know who may have a seizure out there, I don't know who will sprain an ankle, miles from help. Our hike leaders are kids: will they all have good judgment if something goes wrong?

"I will not take a relaxed breath till they *all* come back. You will not be able to tell, but I will be a nervous wreck until these students are back here at Bread Loaf, every single one of them."

Everyone made it back. After dinner, we had a square dance with the Will Dicker Boys calling and playing.

The most dramatic image I have of that Bread Loaf Orientation was late one night when we had a powerful electrical storm. A nearby lightning strike, illuminating the whole landscape, was followed immediately by KABOOM! thunder, again and again. Students sat on the porches of their dorms and enjoyed the show for nearly an hour.

I was at Frothingham Cabin with other staff members and could hear students applauding, cheering the natural fireworks show they were witnessing.

Pink Slip

No one could have come in under better auspices than Tim Light.
His inauguration in the fall of 1990 was splendid. The whole
faculty, staff, and student body walked to the Field House from
the town green, the faculty in academic regalia. Music. Dancing.
Townspeople lined the streets. It was like a medieval gala.

As a scholar of Chinese language and culture, Light presented
to the world a kind of Eastern equanimity. His manner was
humble and self-effacing. His style was in marked contrast to
his predecessor, Olin Robison, who enjoyed being the center of
attention.

He was not what he seemed to be. In his relations with his staff,
he was austere and unpleasant.

He created a budget shortfall at Middlebury right away. We
would get smaller and leaner. "I've seen what's going to happen
to Middlebury because I've been there," he once said to me. He
determined Middlebury would be going the route of Kalamazoo
College, from whence he had been plucked to be our president.
In President's Staff meetings on Tuesday mornings, he would
occasionally just get up and leave the room. Once when he did
this, one of the vice presidents sat back and said, "Okay, who's
got the cards?"

When my turn came at these meetings, as we went around the
table, I would report on the weekend fraternity activities. This
was the final year of fraternities at Middlebury and they were not
going quietly.

President Light would interrogate me with cryptic questions and responses. Understanding what he expected of me as dean of students was "harder than Chinese algebra," as Tom Waits said.

After one exchange, I was totally exasperated. "Tim," I said in frustration, "I have no idea what you're talking about. I can work on a team. I can take direction, but I don't have a clue what you expect from me." The room was silent. I had violated the customary decorum. The usual tone was polite and formal. Emotion was rare.

Maggie O'Brien, associate vice president for sciences, came down to my office later to check in. She was already headed out the door to become President of Hollins College the next year. "That was great," she said effusively. "You spoke for all of us."

"Yeah," I said, "great at pounding nails into my own coffin."

When he scheduled an appointment for me in his office for a one-hour lunch meeting, one flight up in Old Chapel, in January, the handwriting was on the wall.

The pink slip was okay with me. I couldn't imagine working further for Tim Light. He had lost my respect.

He outlined the shifting of my duties at the end of the spring semester: more teaching, study abroad advising, overseeing academic advising.

Fine with me.

Still, my ambition was modest enough: my highest professional aspiration was to be the dean of students at Middlebury or another good place. I wouldn't have minded a longer run.

I wish I could have foreseen that the trustees were going to pull the plug on Tim Light's presidency after only one year.

President and Mrs. Light: Inaugural Parade, Fall 1990

Time Bomb

I was working at my desk one morning that fall when Tim Light appeared at my door. He entered and tossed a piece of paper on my desk. "Have you seen this?" he asked.

I had. It was a letter to me, a long letter, with a copy to the President, from the head of the court diversion program in town.

It might be a stretch to say that letter got me fired from the dean's job, but it certainly didn't help.

She wrote in this letter, which ran to three or four pages, that students who had gone through her diversion program (students caught with fake IDs in local watering holes) said that the College didn't care whether underage students drank illegally. Her evidence was a presentation I made during Orientation, as it had been described to her by students in Court Diversion.

It was a good talk. I was proud of it. I gave it on the students' first night here—that timing underscoring the seriousness, I thought, of the alcohol situation on campus.

It was thorough and straightforward, not patronizing. I talked about the law and the College's responsibility to respect it. It had a policy component and an educational component. I spoke about the danger of alcohol consumption, episodically and over time. I cited studies (Wechsler, Harvard) that showed first-year students to be at special risk. I presented information gleaned from surveys by our own alcohol educator, Yonna McShane.

I didn't talk down to them. I actually thought that understanding the alcohol issues on campus was a particular strength. I had chaired two alcohol committees and written the final committee reports. The recommendations had largely been accepted and implemented by the College. I certainly had enough experience. I used to call myself the "Dean of Beer."

This acknowledgment that underage freshmen drank formed the basis of the contention that the College and the Dean "didn't care" about the law.

So I told the president that I had read the letter and would draft a thoughtful response that night. I didn't see it as a crisis. I said I would explain what our policy and approach was. I looked forward to clearing the air and responding to her concerns.

"You'll do no such thing," he said. "This is a 'time bomb.' John Emerson will deal with this." John, a math professor, was dean of the College. John responded to the letter by suggesting a series of meetings between us and town authorities. We met with the court diversion volunteers.

Nothing much changed. Students still drank too much, especially first-years.

I missed Olin Robison.

I called myself the "Dean of Beer" the 15 years
I was in the Dean of Students Office. It was a joke, sort of.

Lucky Man

After my fateful meeting with Tim light, I was low.

I knew that new presidents often shuffled the deck, but couldn't help feeling that I had at some level failed.

Just a day of two after the announcement of the change of duties, I bumped into Don Wyatt of the history department on the path from Old Chapel to Mead Chapel.

Don had spent a couple of years as dean of the College so had some awareness of the student affairs landscape.

"You must be the happiest guy in the world," he said.

"How's that?"

He explained, "No more late nights at frat houses corralling drunks, no more dealing with police, no more hospital crises— you're a lucky man."

I was taken aback and only could offer a lame, "Well, somebody's got to do it, and I'm good at it."

I wondered, "Is that what the faculty believed? That this job, dean of students, is a default position for people who don't know better, who can't do anything else, who are gluttons for punishment?"

My Affair

During that Tim Light year, 1990–91, I was called into campus after midnight on at least a couple dozen occasions—it seemed like every weekend.

Fraternities totally ignored the rules about closing time of parties. Frustrated townspeople called the State Police. Invariably, Campus Security Director Pete Chenevert gave me a call, and I headed, per his instructions, to a frat party of 100–200 revelers, and attempted, with him, to keep the lid on.

That was the routine.

In their anger and frustration, the frats thought they had little to lose. "What are you going to do, shut us down?" On party nights they had strength in numbers.

As the face of the administration that had consigned them to history, I also received anonymous calls on the weekends in the early morning hours. Drunk, the callers would not remember what they said in the morning, but I would. Sleep was in short supply.

One night that last year, I was awakened from sleep at about 2:00 a.m. by a call from Pete, asking me to come in and give him and his officers a hand with a party at DU.

I turned to Brett and said, "I have to go in." Then I joked about the frequency of these early morning adventures. "You probably think I'm having an affair."

"Yeah," she said, "with Pete."

Beer Tent

Ann Hanson and I are friends. She succeeded me as dean and served as dean of student affairs from 1991 to 2009. For some of those years, I reported to her.

The transition at times was a little rocky, especially early. As dean of advising and off-campus study, I assumed some prerogatives in the dean of students' operation that I perhaps shouldn't have.

I can't deny I would have liked a longer run as dean of students. Tim Light! But . . . the College took care of me, and I think as "Dean of This 'n That" I worked hard and made a contribution.

That's the legacy of my dad, Dean Lindholm at Bates. Living through the Depression, he always emphasized that if I had a job not to take it lightly, and to give my employer a good day's work for a day's pay.

In the aftermath of Tim Light's reshuffling, my dad's voice was often present.

As for my relationship with Ann, it really helped that her son Matt was best friend's with my son David. How can you have a hard time with the mom of your son's best friend? Dave views Ann as almost a second (well, technically third) mom.

On Reunion Weekends these days, Ann and I go together to the Saturday gala when all the classes are together under their tents. We stand there at the beer tent and people who like us, who remember us fondly, come by and visit.

The ice is broken—we have fun. In my case, for those frat guys whose recollection is not so positive, I'm easy to avoid.

Ann mentored three Posse cohorts (Posse is a scholarship and leadership program for students from a particular city who attend Middlebury and other colleges as a group).

Hitched

On a Thursday afternoon in October at 4:00 p.m., Brett came by Old Chapel after her office hours and we walked together to the Chaplain's House on South Street to get married.

Gary Margolis, my college roommate, colleague at Middlebury, and dear friend, stood by me; Judy Liskin-Gasparro of the Spanish Department was Brett's witness. Chaplain John Walsh officiated as Brett and I exchanged our vows. Then we all went to Mister Ups.

Nobody but us knew we were married. I loved that. No fuss. And everyone found out soon enough.

The next month, in November 1990, we had a big party in the newly renovated McCullough social space, with Big Joe Burrell and the Unknown Blues Band providing the music. A good time was had by all.

Twenty-six years. So far. So good.

Brett and Karl, 1990

"Hans"

Dave Rahr was one of my all-time favorite colleagues—not just mine, everyone liked Dave. A genial fellow with a great sense of humor, he was the director of development at the College, then left that job to lead for another decade and a half the Vermont Community Foundation in Middlebury.

I met Dave one evening when we were both in the checkout line at Grand Union in town. I was buying a bottle of champagne and a dozen roses. Dave asked about the occasion I was obviously celebrating.

Brett had just polished the final, final copy of her wonderful biography of the poet Elizabeth Bishop and sent it off to her publisher, the University of California Press.

"My wife just finished her book," I said proudly, "took her 10 years."

"Slow reader," he said, without missing a beat.

Another time when I bumped into him and he asked what was up, I told him, "I got a dog for my wife."

"Good swap," he said.

He had a joke file in his office, the contents of which he would occasionally share with visitors. It was full of clippings from newspapers and magazines that his friends all over the country sent him that were unintentionally hilarious.

Dave's son Tim is a Middlebury graduate (1989) and his grandson, Tom, is in the class of 2020. I called Tim "Hans" for two years by mistake before I learned his real name.

When Tim was a freshman, I was invited to join an intramural basketball team, an offer I was happy to accept. At the first game, I was introduced to my teammates, including a tall slender blond boy, "Hans."

I had a good time playing with these guys and had the occasion to call out to Hans often in the course of the games we played.

When I saw him on campus, I naturally greeted him warmly — "hello, Hans." He always returned my greeting. I called him "Hahns," as I thought that was more ethnically appropriate than the nasally "Hans" of his friends.

After some time, either he or his friends mercifully set me straight. "Hans" was a nickname and it was not "Hahns," it was "Hands," a derogatory (but affectionate) nickname, short for "Bad Hands" or "No Hands," based on his inability in basketball to catch the ball cleanly or dribble it.

Now Tim has a boy at Middlebury, Tom, and I don't know if he has good hands, but I had him in class and I know he's smart.

Not Harvard

My daughter Jane went to Harvard because she got in. Students don't turn down Harvard.

Her people were all from Bates and Middlebury, so the sink-or-swim atmosphere of Harvard was a big adjustment.

In the fall of her freshman year she came home to visit during a break. I invited her to attend my first-year seminar, an examination of the Yankee archetype, in a course called "Roads Less Traveled: Literature and Culture of Northern New England." It was a particularly good, lively class that year.

That evening Jane and I went to a hockey game at Kenyon Arena. As we were standing just inside the doors, figuring out where to sit, students from the class, two ebullient girls, approached us and said, "Hi, Jane, come with us," and Jane happily complied.

She told me later, "That would never happen at Harvard."

She appreciated the easy social graces of Middlebury students. I don't think it's breeding. I think there's something in the atmosphere at Middlebury that encourages warmth and cordiality.

Science Writer

What in the world would we talk about?

Brett and I were the first Faculty Heads of Atwater Commons in our new Commons System in 1991. The College had provided us with a beautiful home on Weybridge Street. We were expected to entertain. We hadn't started a family. We had a big house; the more the merrier.

One of our first guests was Dava Sobel, who was the science

writer for the *New York Times* and *The New Yorker*. She had written a best-seller, *Longitude*, about clock-maker John Harrison who invented the clock that helped establish longitude and latitude lines, thus allowing mariners to survive in long cross-ocean voyages. It was about Greenwich Mean Time.

Now I know that explanation makes little sense. I am not a science guy; I was not a good science student in high school, though I was earnest. I'm easily confused. I read the book, but it largely eluded me, as I recall.

Sobel wrote other successful books, including *Galileo's Daughter*, which is about, well, Galileo's daughter. Middlebury awarded Sobel an Honorary Degree in 2002. So I was intimidated, to say the least. She was staying with us for two nights and I was her host.

She arrived a few hours before her lecture and we chatted in the kitchen: the usual small talk—that was about all I could muster.

Along the way, I told her I was from Lewiston, Maine, where Bates College was located.

She said, "I know all about Bates. When I was younger I lived with a guy who taught at Bates. I worked at WCBB (Colby-Bates-Bowdoin), the public radio station in central Maine, studios in Lewiston."

That was interesting. "Where did you live in Lewiston?"
"Actually," she said, "I lived in Auburn, right over the river."

I knew Auburn too. "Where in Auburn?"

"Cushman Place. 13 Cushman Place."

I was floored. "No way!" I exclaimed. That was where my mother lived, growing up. That precise house.

I told her about my mother's interesting family history, how her family was wealthy, her dad owning a shoe factory in Auburn, but how he lost his business in the Depression and my mother had to come home from Wheaton College to attend Bates as a day student and help her stepmom care for her eight younger siblings. That's how she met my dad, at Bates.

Dava told me about her interesting family as well. We were almost late to her reading.

Like I said—nothing at all in common.

Dr. Baseball

On occasion, I am asked to speak to groups about baseball.

I was presenting a slide show on "Baseball in Vermont" at Project Independence, a day program for the elderly.

I focused the talk on the three greatest Vermont major leaguers: Ray Fisher from Middlebury, Ray Collins from Colchester, and Larry Gardner from Enosburg Falls, who all played at the same time, 1910–20. Gardner is in the Red Sox Hall of Fame.

Fisher went to Middlebury; Collins and Gardner played for UVM and then on the Red Sox teams of Babe Ruth.

Ray Collins' daughter, in her 80s, attended my presentation. At its conclusion, she reminisced about growing up on the farm in

Colchester. "I remember one day my dad came in the kitchen and asked my mom, 'What happened to that Red Sox jacket up in the attic. It's not there.'

"My mom said, 'That ratty old thing? I threw it away.'

"'That's too bad,' my dad said. 'It belonged to Babe Ruth. Had his name stitched into it. He gave it to me.'"

Then she turned to me and asked, "Do you think that would be worth anything today?"

Ray Fisher, class of 1910, won 100 games in the major leagues

Saving a Life

Bill Lee was not the only baseball figure to be a guest in my baseball class. He was the only one who became a regular. Dan Duquette also paid us a visit.

Some of you no doubt recognize the name. At present, he pulls the strings for the Baltimore Orioles Baseball Club as their General Manager. For nine years, (199–2002), he was the GM of the Red Sox.

As he is a New England boy (western Massachusetts) who attended Amherst College, I thought he might be intrigued by my academic approach to baseball, so I wrote him an informative letter with an invitation to visit class.

I picked up the ringing phone one day at my desk some weeks later and heard Duquette's unmistakable baritone, recognizable from all the times I had heard him speak on the radio or TV before or after a Red Sox game. I was pleasantly surprised.

We arranged a date for him to come after the season. As it turned out, he had to cancel at the last minute as he had just traded for Pedro Martinez and had scheduled a press conference to introduce him to Boston media. I gave him a Dean's Excuse and we settled on an alternate date.

In the meantime, however, he got fired! The Red Sox had been purchased by a new ownership group in January of 2002 and made replacing the GM just about their first order of business. While Duquette's tenure had been successful overall, his departure was not met with howls of protest in Beantown. The 2001 season had been fraught with controversy.

I asked if he would speak in a public setting to anyone who would like to come, but he declined, so the students in my class and many of their friends settled into a large classroom in our new (at the time) science building.

Those who are familiar with the public Duquette know that he does not have an effusive personality — far from it: he is laconic. He does have a sense of humor, though of the Yankee variety, understated, ironic.

He gave us a fairly dry dissertation on the business of baseball, referring to the players as "assets" and talking about "maximizing revenues," and so on. Near then end of his remarks, he talked somewhat more personally about his job running the Red Sox and its challenges.

He told us about the tensions, the stresses of the job, and how he dealt with them. He said that he came to enjoy going for a sail on game days on the Charles River that separates Boston from Cambridge, only a stone's throw from Kenmore Square and Fenway Park.

He was not an experienced sailor, but a couple of hours on the Charles in a little sailboat on nice summer day brought him to the park relaxed and more ready to face the challenges of running the Red Sox with its avid fan base.

One day, however, he told us, he got in trouble. Coming about, he lost his balance and was pitched over the side. Underwater, he couldn't untangle himself from the ropes, try as he might, and swim to the surface.

This was bad. He was convinced he was going to drown.

Next thing he knew, still attached to the ropes, he was being pulled up through the water. When he got to the surface, he saw he had been saved by three boys, teenagers, who had seen his distress from their sailboat.

They very likely had saved his life, and Duquette was grateful indeed. He asked what he might do for them.

The first boy said, "You're Dan Duquette, right?" Duquette acknowledged as much. "Do you think you could get my family Red Sox season tickets?"

"For saving my life? Absolutely!"

The next boy thought for a minute, "Can I have a Nomar Garciaparra jersey with all the Red Sox players' autographs on it?"

"No problem," Duquette said.

The students in my class were silent, attentive, transfixed by this dramatic account.

The last boy thought for a long time, before saying, "Okay, here's what I want: when I die, will you spread my ashes on the pitcher's mound at Fenway?"

"Of course," Duquette said. "But you're just a kid, isn't there something I can do for you now? Why do you want me to spread your ashes in Fenway Park?"

"Because when I go home and tell my dad that I saved Dan Duquette's life, he's gonna kill me!"

A good story. Well played, Dan Duquette.

The Walk of Shame

One Winter Term I was asked by Ana Martinez-Lage of the Spanish department to discuss academic advising (I was dean of advising, after all) with the class for new faculty she was organizing that year. I had done this before and was always glad to discuss the importance of academic advising.

I filed the time and date and resolved to make a compelling presentation.

When the day came, I forgot all about the meeting, didn't show up, blew it off, screwed up. I was not out carousing, just didn't look at my schedule that morning, and sat at my desk doing something else at the appointed hour.

Maybe the people who took note of my organizational weaknesses had a point.

I didn't realize my delinquency until I left work and stopped to get some gas on my way home at the end of the day at Maplefield's on the edge of town. I pulled up to the gas pump and saw Ana filling her tank right in front of me.

Oh no! Sheesh. Dumbass. I realized what I had done, or had failed to do. I got out of the car and prostrated myself, profuse with my apologies, extravagant in my guilt. She was kind (kinder than I would have been), not such a big deal, finished up, and drove off.

I got back in my car, relieved, but still guilt-ridden and shaken. Soon enough I headed home.

That's right: gas pump hose still in the tank.
I drove to Fire & Ice before I realized all the people honking and waving at me weren't just happy to see me.

I never knew what a long walk it was from Fire & Ice to Maplefield's until I did it carrying 15 feet of a gas pump.

I only felt a little better when I told my story to my colleague Sue Ritter and she described for me the time she drove from Middlebury all the way to Bethel, Vermont, and the entrance to the thruway there, 50 miles from Middlebury, before realizing that she was trailing the gas hose from her tank.

Times Change

One of my favorite quotations is from "Pat Garrett and Billy the Kid" when the Kid (played by Bob Dylan!) says "Times change, but I don't."

Of course, he says this shortly before he dies.

Amid the chaos of the Vietnam War era, I also wanted to be steady, reliable, unchanging: what you see is what you get—a very Yankee view. I would not be buffeted by whimsy, fashion, or fad. That was my thinking.

John McCardell, President of Middlebury from 1992–2004 and a big-time agent of change, once declared that "Sometimes the *appearance* of change is as good as change itself."

Boy, I took him to task for that, objecting strongly to the suggestion that appearances were a measure of quality, or vitality, in an institution. No, I told him we should find what is real, and enduring, indeed what works!

McCardell tried to tell us that the times they were a-changing. He wanted Middlebury to cease being content as "middle"bury and dare to display ambition; he didn't want us to be "big"bury, but rather "best"bury, or at least "better-than-we-are"bury. He forced change on us, some us kicking and screaming.

President John McCardell

His vision was pretty much opposite of Tim Light's, who wanted to make Middlebury lean and mean, a good buy, with fewer students. John said, in effect, "Nay, we'll get bigger not smaller. Our program is too big for our enrollment. Applications rise every year; we can absorb the increase."

Money was out there in the 1990s and McCardell spent it. We built buildings: academic buildings—an enormous science center, a new library, and athletic facilities—a swimming pool (natatorium) and a hockey rink, all state of the art.
He said we should go after Williams and Amherst and the Ivies.
He overwhelmed my (and others') conservative instincts.

Sure looks now like he knew what he was doing.

Four Divas

The phone rang at about 5:00 a.m., waking me up. It was David Edleson, dean of Cook Commons, with terrible, terrible news.

Four young women, first-years, had been killed in a single car crash a few hours before. They were coming back from Montreal in the early morning when the driver evidently fell asleep and crashed into a bridge abutment at full highway speed.

Four beautiful and talented young women, all students of color, all friends. They were special, poised for success: the word was out. They would make their mark. They would change Middlebury College by the force of their talent and energy. They themselves believed it and relished the challenge of helping to transform this place, their new home, and many others were beginning to realize that their presence would be transforming.

We believed this despite the fact that they had only been at Middlebury for a few months.

Kathy Ebner, director of residential life, Frank Kelley's protégé and successor, was in charge of the College's response to this awful situation.

She assembled about two dozen of us that morning, all desperate to help: deans of commons, faculty heads, the chaplain, and others in student affairs who were close to students and fell generally under Kathy's supervision.

We crowded into the conference room in Adirondack House, shocked and saddened, and she coordinated our response, being both attentive to suggestion and authoritative when need be.

Two of the Four Divas, Iniko and Maika

Kathy was magnificent in this crisis, calm and confident. I will admire her forever for the humane, compassionate, and utterly capable way she orchestrated the aftermath of this tragedy. The College is in her debt for her extraordinary professionalism in this dramatic case.

She asked Brett and me to host the mother of one of the students, Maika Prewitt, from St. Louis, at our College house, Nichols House, on Weybridge Street. She would stay with us. We were to attend to her needs as best we could.

She was a single mother. Maika was her only child, the light of her life, her best friend. She had seen her off to college in another part of the country five months before, and now in the middle of her first year far away from her home and her mom, she was dead. Maika was the driver of the car.

Our hearts reached out to Maika's mom. Vulnerable in her grief, she was appreciative of anything done for her, crushed by the burden of her loss. Other faculty heads in Commons houses were hosting the other grieving families.

We were so thankful for these spaces, not hotel rooms, but homes, where parents and siblings and other grieving family members could be in a warm and supportive setting.

Kathy Ebner

The next days and weeks were a time of overwhelming emotion on campus. The memorial service was heartbreaking.

Then they all left, and we, the living, got on with our busy lives, sadder, maybe wiser, who knows.

It is ever thus.

Commons Slut

I have a distinction that I think no one else at Middlebury will ever have: I was a faculty head or a dean in all five of our residential commons.

I was faculty head of Atwater Commons with Brett for the first eight years of the system. Then I became the Commons' pinch-hitter deluxe.

I was the interim faculty head in Ross for a year while they went about finding another. Then I did the same thing in Brainerd on two occasions. In 2007, Matt Longman, dean of Wonnacott Commons went on "family leave" for the fall and I stood in for him. My last gig was as Cook Commons dean in 2008, when the Cook dean resigned in August, too late to mount a search for his replacement.

The understanding was that I would do my pinch-hitter thing in Cook until they could undertake a real search. But the economy tanked—the College instituted a hiring freeze and I was asked to stay on. They didn't need the hard sell: I liked it.

I retired in January, 2011, as part of the College's voluntary retirement plan: the College offered a lot of money if you promised to stop working. Seemed like a good deal to me. I had kids in high school and a wife working full time who could use some relief from the practical routines.

I wasn't by myself in retiring. Gary Margolis did too—he was director of the Counseling Office for 38 years. Also, a dozen tenured faculty members.

I mentioned this accidental accomplishment of leadership in all five commons to a group of students and one said, "You're just a commons slut! You'll do it with any commons."

A Little Night Music

"Are you having any fun?" I asked Anywhere Sikochi, a first-year student from Zimbabwe, class of 2005. That was his name, "Anywhere," but he preferred "Siko." He was one of the 175 international students from 66 countries at Middlebury.

Siko was taking a challenging course load, and working ten to 20 hours a week in a number of jobs. On top of the enormous cultural adjustment, I was concerned that his life at Middlebury allowed for little or no leisure time.

"Oh yes," he said. "I belong to a singing and running group." He went on to describe Mchakamchaka (pronounced how it looks—"mmm-chaka. . . mmm-chaka"), an organization of students who gathered twice a week at night to sing and run.

They sang African choral music, running songs from Tanzania

and other parts of southern Africa, songs of the Nguni and Bantu people and regions, in the languages of Zulu, Xhosa ("Ko-sa"), Shona, and Kiswahili. If you know Ladysmith Black Mambazo or Miriam Makeba, you know the sound.

That very night after my conversation with Siko, I came into campus for a Brainerd Commons Council meeting. At the meeting's end, about 10:15 p.m., I was walking to my car when I heard the captivating cadences of Mchakamchaka for myself.

A group of 15–20 shadowy figures were coming toward me on Proctor Road running at a fairly good clip, singing, loud and strong, a rhythmic song.

Their song, their activity, was a celebration, an unmistakably joyous sound, cutting through the darkness and chill of a late February night in Vermont. The moment took up just that, about a moment, but I was transfixed, thrilled. It was so cool.

I raced home and called my son, David, also a first-year student at Middlebury, and left him a message on his voice-mail, telling him of my discovery of Mchakamchaka.

I came to work the next morning to find a message on my machine from David: "Too late, Dad," he said. "You missed me last night because I was out running . . . and singing. I do it every week. It's great." David had already discovered Mchakamchaka.

Mchakamchaka was the result of a serendipitous encounter of a student from Appleton, Maine, with another from Mwanza, Tanzania, who arrived at Middlebury at the same time to start college in February 2001.

Bennett Konesni, the Maine boy, fell in love with African choral music in high school. "In my senior year in high school, we spent the whole year in chorus singing African music in preparation for a three-week trip to South Africa. I developed a passion for African choral music and came to Middlebury with a library of African music."

The student from Tanzania was Kiddo ("Kee-doe") Kidolezi. They were assigned a room together. They also found themselves in the same First-Year Seminar, Art and Chemistry, with Professor SunHee Choi.

Kiddo and Bennett (and Sarah Holland) lead Mchakamchaka in their nocturnal run and sing through the campus

On Monday and Thursday nights, Middlebury Mchakamchaka gathered at Gifford Hall at 10:00 p.m., and ran and sang for about 45 minutes.

Anybody could join in. Nearly 40 students, men and women alike, became members. Three of the students were from Africa.

At the end of every nocturnal run, the group always sang a parting song. They circled around a maple tree between Mead Chapel and Gifford Hall and sang "Shosholoza."

"It's everyone's favorite song," said Bennett. "It's beautiful. No one wants to leave."

Flying Bula

"Are you paying my son to play ice hockey?" I asked Bob Smith, the director of intramurals at Middlebury.

"Absolutely, and happy to do it," he responded.

"Isn't that an NCAA violation?"

"Have you seen him play?"

David was the commissioner of the Intramural Ice Hockey League at the College his senior year.

As commissioner, he made schedules, kept records, handed out helmets, resolved an occasional dispute. He was at the rink when there were games and oversaw the action.

He kept his skates on so if a team were shorthanded, he played. Otherwise, he sat in the penalty box and did his homework.

Though he was born in Middlebury, David never learned how to skate until he came back to go to college. He lived with his mother in Boston during the school year and became a fan of the game if not a participant.

I remember the first College game he saw as a three-year old in the frigid Duke Nelson Arena. He was transfixed when the teams first came out on the ice in their colorful uniforms and skated circles around the rink, really fast.

The first check in the game, right in front us, a defenseman slamming an attacker into the boards, made him jump. When his mother asked him after the game what he liked best, he said, "Crashing into the glass."

His spring breaks in Vermont always seemed to coincide with Middlebury's annual run to the National Championship in men's hockey. From ages 11 to 15, he saw the Championship games, all Middlebury wins. He even took the trip to Plattsburgh in a blizzard in 1998.

He was very proud of his intramural "B" League team, Flying Bula, winner of the league in 2002, ("We'd get crushed in 'A' League"). The core of the team was together for three years.

"Bula" is a Fijian word that means many things—hello, good-bye, I love you, like the word "Aloha" in Hawaiian. At least that's what David claimed.

David was the "Coach," so he sometimes wore a sport coat when he played. They also had a general manager, a director of hockey operations (they called him the "Doho"), and a captain, Max Jones, the team's organizational genius and progenitor.

They had beautiful hockey jerseys, patterned after the old Red Army uniforms. Bula was written in Cyrillic in the front below a hammer and sickle. So much for the Cold War.

Players had their names and numbers on their back. There were some duplicate numbers ("Who cares?") David's name was Karetov, which roughly translated to "Coach," or "Son of Coach"; The Doho, Jeff Stauch, was "Staucharianov." Max Jones was "Maxyzch." Former Middlebury resident, Buck Sleeper, had "Buckov" on the back of his shirt.

The season lasted from late November to Winter Carnival in February. Some weeks David was in Nelson four nights. I asked him about his schoolwork.

"Dad," he said, "This is my *job!*"

*David '05
and Jane*

Professor Lindholm?

Who doesn't belong and why?

Professor Brett Millier
Professor John Elder
Professor Murray Dry
Professor Allison Stanger
Professor Karl Lindholm

Karl Lindholm? In that company? Pardon me.

Getting a PhD was a happy accident—and the luckiest, or perhaps smartest, thing I could have done. When I outgrew my usefulness in certain positions—dean of students and study abroad adviser, for example, I could move into the classroom without causing too much embarrassment to the College. ("Well, he *does* have a PhD").

There were times when getting the doctorate seemed like a fool's errand: I didn't need the degree—a master's was sufficient at the time, that's what Erica Wonnacott had. Jody and I had started a family and burning the midnight oil working on a dissertation after a long day in the dean of students office was hard to justify.

My last decade and a half I was a true hybrid—half student-affairs as the dean of advising with duties in the commons system and half-faculty, teaching a first year seminar in the fall and a 2IU class (two instructional units—that is, a big class, over 40 students) in the spring.

I knew I had come into the faculty through the side door. I would not have been invited to join the faculty in an open search. That's not modesty, trust me. I read the dossiers of those seeking teaching positions in American studies and American literature. I would not have been given a second look.

I took on more teaching duties after we made the switch in the dean of students office. The first day of class the next year, fall 1991—I was teaching a First-Year Seminar—was very hot. I had on a light blue shirt and a tie. I was anxious, perspiring profusely. Big dark splotches appeared on my shirt.

Just before class I ran home (it wasn't far, just a few hundred yards to Nichols House, the Atwater Commons Faculty Head residence) and changed into a navy blue polo shirt that wouldn't show the sweat. After 10–15 minutes in class I relaxed and it was okay.

I was comfortable being "Dean" Lindholm, who taught on the side, no sweat.

"Professor" Lindholm? Now that was another matter.

Cellphone

I was in class, making a brilliant point, I'm sure, before dozens of rapt students, when a phone rang, a cellphone.

Don't you just hate that? It's always an annoyance, disruptive of any rhythm or atmosphere. I had certainly glanced askance, if not worse, at students whose phone went off in class.

It rang again.

I realized it was *my* phone, in my pants pocket. How could that be? Nobody ever called me. The only people with my number were members of my immediate family, and they rarely called because they knew I was unreliable: I was prone to leaving my phone in my car or in my desk or in my pocket uncharged or turned off for days at a time.

It was my daughter, Annie, 11 years old at the time, home from school, sick. She didn't realize I was in class.

This was the daughter who once called me when I was in Phoenix watching Middlebury spring-trip baseball and asked me for a ride home from Middlebury Middle School. I had been gone *three days*. "Sorry, Dad. I forgot."

What the heck, I thought, class is blown, so I broke one of my own cardinal rules: I took the call. Might as well have some fun. I put it on speaker phone. I would give the students a glimpse of what awaits them when they are parents (I was 64 at the time).

"Hi, Annie. What's up?"

"Can I buy a pay-per-view movie?"

"I don't know. What movie?"

It was the Sherlock Holmes movie with Robert Downey Jr. It was PG 13, very different from the Holmes movies I knew. This one had darkness and violence, scary moments, and she was home alone, not feeling well. I genuinely didn't know if watching this movie was a good idea.

"I don't know, Annie. Let's put it to a vote." She realized then she was on speaker phone.

"Dad!"

"How many think this is a suitable video for an eleven-year-old?" I asked the class. Lots of hands went up.

"Who think she's too young?" just a few hands.

"Okay, Annie. Buy the movie."

Class resumed, with students I suspect glad for the interlude. Annie was annoyed with me, but she got her way.

Destination Point

I liked all the offices I had in my three-and-half decades working for the College. I loved that Dean of Students complex right at the core of Old Chapel on the second floor, and my office too in Adirondack with my American Studies colleagues (my wife had the office right next door—that was convenient).

So when Ted Perry, the acting dean of the college in 2007–08, asked me to move into the new Library, I was hesitant. I liked where I was.

It turned out this was a good deal for me—a brand new spacious office that I could configure as I chose on the main floor of a beautiful new building.

Ted explained that we wanted to ensure the new library was actually used by students, by moving a number of operations there that guaranteed traffic: the Computer Help Desk, the Center for Teaching, Learning, and Research (CTLR), the video collection, a café.

He said, "Karl, you see lots of students as dean of advising; we consider you a destination point."

Okay. I liked that. I moved and thought about signing my correspondence thereafter:

"Karl Lindholm, Destination Point."

Love Letters

I never really received any "hate" mail as one of the Deans of Students or Commons.

There was that letter to Tim Light about alcohol policy from the court diversion person, but that wasn't personal. And one of my fraternity brothers cited some comments of mine about the fraternity situation as especially objectionable in a letter to President Robison that Olin shared with me.

There were those hate calls from the frat boys, but (intoxicated) they knew not what they were doing.

Fred Neuberger told me once that he kept a file of "love letters." These were letters of thanks or appreciation to him for doing his job in Admissions. He said, "I don't believe most of them, but I keep them in case I need them."

I kept them too. I keep everything. I have numerous files, boxes of letters and cards, many in long-hand. Of course, all these letters stop in the mid-1990s, when so much of our correspondence became electric. I keep files on my computer now, but I can't find anything. It's hard not to feel a loss.

Here's the nicest letter I ever received. It's beautifully handwritten in blue ink on two index cards that the author had enhanced by drawing a simple design, filigree, on the edges. I didn't mind she spelled my name wrong.

Dear Carl,

I would like to thank you for your kindness, understanding, and support. I had never been in such a vulnerable position as I was at the beginning of this fall, and I was nervous about making a room change. But from the moment I stepped into your office I felt like you were genuinely concerned with my situation, and you made me feel comfortable, safe, and cared for. Where I could have been met with obstacles I was met with helping hands that allowed me to make necessary changes quickly and start to get on with my life. Thank you for helping make this rough time smoother. I will never forget the attention and care you gave me when I needed it most.

—Most Sincerely,

I didn't get notes like that every day.

I really hadn't done anything that special. I had authorized a room change, by-passing the red-tape that accompanies most requests. Karin Hall-Kolts, our Director of Housing, assigned her a new room, that day. It was lucky we had an open room available.

In room draw the previous spring, she had chosen a room in Forest Hall next door to her Middlebury boyfriend of two years.

Then, that fall, they broke up. The proximity of their rooms was awkward and extremely painful, on both sides, impossible really.

She had waited to come in, not expecting to be taken seriously ("I broke up with my boyfriend," how cliché, she figured). Her presentation of the situation was without histrionics, but was very compelling. I was reminded of a painful a breakup of my own early in my time as a student at Middlebury, in a relationship not nearly as serious as the one she described to me. I let her jump the line.

The next day I received her card.

Her former boyfriend left school at the end of the semester, took the spring off, and finished the next fall, after she had graduated.

We sometimes forget that young love can be pretty serious business too.

Creepy Guy

Route 125, College Street extension, heading west from the campus, is a dangerous road. It's narrow, the speed limit is 50, and has two blind hills. Anyone driving on it must be attentive. Students running, biking, or roller-blading really need to be careful—and they aren't.

In the late afternoon, in spring and fall, the sun setting in the west severely limits the visibility of drivers heading that way.

In the nice weather, when people are zooming home, the road is full of students getting some exercise. Routes 125 and 30 (Main Street) are connected by Cider Mill Road, where I live with Brett, Peter and Annie, and dogs. It's about a five-mile loop. When I was in college we called it the "Triangle." Cider Mill Road is the hypotenuse.

One day in the spring I was driving home, sun in my eyes, and two Middlebury students, women, appeared, running side-by-side, chatting, coming over one of those hills, oblivious the danger of oncoming traffic.

"That's so dangerous!" I thought. "They should be more careful." I decided to go back and tell them to be more careful. After all, that's what deans do: tell students to be careful.

So I turned around and drove slowly back, got close to the young women, and lowered my window. Before I could state my concern, they sped up.

As they ran away, I yelled, "No, no, I just want to talk to you."

That didn't help. Full sprint now.

I drove straight to Campus Security and told the dispatcher, "If two students come and say some creepy guy is harassing women running on 125 . . . it's me."

Hoop Crazy

I begged my kids to come to Middlebury sports events with me.

When a dad takes his kids to a game, he's a good dad. If he goes by himself and leaves the kids at home, he's borderline selfish.

My son Peter often agreed to come along to College basketball games, and I rarely missed a home game. But he would bring a *Harry Potter* book, and when things got too noisy and intense in the game, he would retire to Lawson Lounge to read in peace. He especially despised the buzzer that signaled time stoppages or otherwise punctuated play. It made him jump in fright.

Lucky for me, Peter fell in love with basketball in the seventh grade, just as Middlebury was becoming terrific in hoop. We shared a passion for Middlebury basketball, getting to know the players and exulting in their success.

Peter is a wonderful athlete, though not blessed with great natural ability. He loves sports. He earned every minute of playing time he enjoyed on the Middlebury Tiger (high school) basketball and baseball teams.

I told a friend that Peter was on the high school basketball team and he asked, "Do you think he'll play in college?"
I said, "Absolutely. Every day." And he has.
He's not on the Middlebury team—he's not a player at that skill

level—but he loves to play pick-up. He's about my height and has inherited my speed and jumping ability, or lack thereof, (and he does have a nice shot—I may have helped with that).

He plays "noon hoops" in Pepin Gym nearly every day—and whenever else he's free and there's a game going on. He's fit, works out incessantly.

I played noon hoops until I was in my 50s. I too loved pick-up. The noon hoops crowd is a motley crew of all ages (from 18–68), shapes, and abilities—faculty and staff and some locals.

I asked Peter why he likes playing with these old guys and not with his student contemporaries, and he said, "I know there's a game, Dad. I'm busy and I don't have the time to call people and set up a game, or go to the gym and see who's there.

"There's always someone as good as I am for me to guard." So Monday-Wednesday-Friday he plays at noon with the old guard.

On Tuesday and Thursday noons, there's "invitational" hoops with coaches and other members of the athletic department. It's a faster game and Pete is the only student invited to join in.

It's a high honor, and I'm proud of him, for it means that he has embraced the pick-up hoops pristine ethos, which is, "don't be a pain in the . . . neck": don't hog the ball or shoot too much, don't call too many fouls, don't complain, just play.

Good rules for living.

Peter likes to write poems. In his junior year, he had this one in the student arts magazine, called *Blackbird*:

The Faculty Game

In Pepin Gymnasium time backpedals
stumbling clumsily over its worn hightops
as the ball advances towards it.
The clock reads 12:00
but the year could be 1975, 1998, or 2003.
Old men grunt and stomp and sweat
as they did when their bodies were lithe and young.

Time looks on with a grimace
as it nurses a pulled hamstring.

They once howled at the moon outside of bars
and wrapped their arms around soft bare shoulders
before stumbling down sidewalks
in shiny black shoes.

On the court they danced, speaking
in subtle tongues.
The pick and roll, the drive and dish,
they lived and loved.

And then they watched
younger version of themselves
rise as they fell
into the comfortable cradle of fatherhood.
They dance now, but slowly, around Legos
and loose leaf sheets of spelling homework.

They teach the tongues now,
in gruff tones bereft of beauty.
There's enough beauty in the game already.

And time packs up its fragrant gym bag
and heads home.

Noon Hoops: Pete!

Authority

The hardest thing about retirement is the loss of authority, both literal authority in the job and authority in the broadest sense, personal authority. You go from being good at something to not good at much. You stop doing what defined you for so long.

It's important to have a resilient identity. You end up telling a lot of people who you *used* to be.

I was grateful indeed to be able to be a commons dean my last two-and-a-half years. If I hadn't been offered the "buyout" (sorry, Voluntary Retirement Plan) I probably wouldn't have retired, or at least I would have had a tougher decision.

I was 65 years old, had one child in high school, the other in middle school, and a wife who could use a little relief from the myriad daily practical tasks that a family requires.

The Commons Dean job description seemed to be written with me in mind. It liked a dean who taught. For years it seemed I taught *in addition to* full-time work in the deans' office. I liked being a commons dean.

I was lucky. I finished my career, or full-time work anyway, doing something I enjoyed. I didn't limp to the finish line.

Spell-check

I remember watching my dad "dictate" to his secretary, Mrs. Keenan, in his office at Bates College.

She sat in a chair, facing my dad who sat behind his desk and she transcribed in "shorthand" what he said, then produced a draft for him to proof before she typed the final clean draft him to revise. Then she typed a final draft at her desk for him to sign, along with one or two *carbon copies* for the files. I wonder how many young people today can explain the origin of the "cc" at the top of every email we send.

In the early 1990s. I tried twice to learn how to "word process" on the computer. There was still no need. I was comfortable using a "dictaphone," a tape recorder. I would recite my routine correspondence into it, and Peggy Holdman in our office put in her earplugs in and typed it up—a draft first, then a final copy.

I dictated notes like this: "Dear Joe comma. Great to see you exclamation point. I hope you and Susan are well dash and also your children period." And so on. Not that different from my dad. I felt like a Western Union typographer (now there's a period reference).

There are no "secretaries" today. They are "coordinators," highly trained and with a thorough understanding of how computers enhance the effectiveness of teaching and administrative work.

We type our own correspondence and send it out ourselves as email—or print it ourselves and (rarely these days, as we aspire to be a "paperless campus"), write the address on the envelope and send it out, ourselves.

In spring semester, 2009, a young man flunked out—two Fs and a D. I was his dean in Cook Commons and I had never heard of him, no warnings from professors, no visit from him asking for relief. He was a student in Cook Commons, one of mine.

Chagrined, I wrote an email to him, expressing concern and frustration that my interest in him was after-the-fact. He lived in Burlington so I suggested that we get together.

He replied right away and wrote that he'd like to come down to talk to me the very next day.

I emailed right back. I told him that I was busy in the middle of the day, but was free on either end, the morning or mid-afternoon. I would be happy to see him early or later in the day. Then I wrote, or intended to write, "you pick," that is, you *pick* the time of our meeting.

Unfortunately, my clumsy fingers wrote "you prick." Spell-check ignored it. My correspondence ended with "you prick."

Bless his heart, he wrote right back and asked (without copies to the president, dean, or anyone else) if I had intended to write "you prick."

I assured him that indeed I had not.

Happy ending: he took some courses at UVM, did well, and came back to Middlebury and graduated in 2011.

Another email misadventure (there have been many) was when I needed to see a number of students about some problem or another. So I instructed in my emails to make appointments to see me with the Cook Commons Coordinator Linda Schiffer. I wrote in my note, "for a good time, see Linda," meaning a time of mutual convenience.

It wasn't long before Linda came into my office to ask if I wouldn't mind rephrasing. "For a good time, see Linda" sounded, well, a bit too suggestive.

Day Off

Retired now, I enjoy my daily routines.

When I ordered my cheddar dill bagel with bacon and horseradish cream cheese at the Bagel Bakery one morning, I saw my friend Russ Reilly sitting in a booth. So I joined him.

Soon, other retirees, Howard and Bill, joined us. I told Russ I had a busy day ahead: later I was meeting former colleague Matt Longman for coffee at McCullough, and I had a lunch date with old friend and classmate, Rick. At the end of the day, I was going out for a cold one at Two Brothers with another friend.

Russ said, "That's the trouble with retirement—you never get a day off!"

Oh-Oh, Here He Comes

I had seen colleagues who were successful at retirement—and others who were miserable, or at least had trouble adjusting to their irrelevance.

My dad died at 98. He had a 33-year retirement. He and my mom (who died four years after my dad, at 99) lived in Lewiston year-round. Bates was a congenial host to their later years. They preferred winter's blast in Maine to the enervating lifestyle of Florida and other points South and West.

Fred Neuberger and his family were sitting outside the Otter Creek Bakery the morning after he had received the great distinction of an Honorary Degree at Middlebury, his alma mater and employer for more than three decades.

I offered my congratulations on this honor—and Fred responded graciously, then added:

"You do a job for thirty years, and you think you have learned something that may be useful to those who follow you.

"But, you know, the phone never rings."

I figured this would happen in my case, and it has. In my last two and a half years, as dean of Cook Commons, I'd developed relationships with many of the students under my charge, especially the most troubled and fragile ones. I had a sense of their struggles and predilections. The information and insight I had gained would be useful to my successor. But I didn't expect a call, and none came.

Okay with me. I had other plans. I was the same way when I was young in the job. When we take over, young professionals, we want to establish an *original* relationship to our tasks and our constituents. We want to do it our way. We have waited our turn. Our way will be better. It's all designed to be that way. Retire, old fella—and get out of the way.

I am also familiar with people who retire and can't let go. They have time on their hands and are glad to see their friends and former colleagues—who may or may not have time to share.

Change, I have learned, is inevitable, and often means throwing the baby out with the bathwater. Give it up. We had our chance and have to be able to say, "They may be wrong or misguided, but it's their call. I'm out."

In retirement, Duke Nelson was still beloved. Nonetheless, when he approached, his working colleagues would roll their eyes and say, "Gotta run, Duke," because every conversation was a half-hour. It was like that for Fred, too.

That's my worry. I live in fear of "Oh-oh, here he comes."

Brett is something of a recluse. When she comes home at night, we roll up the driveway. She values her private time. My social needs were met during the day, at work, for a long time.

Now I tell people when we talk about having lunch or coffee together: "Monday and Tuesday are good, Wednesday I'm free, and Thursday and Friday will also work. Your call."

When you're retired and you waste a day, it's especially tough because you know that everything you did that day was your choice.

. . . and your days are numbered.

Still Erect

The Saturday morning of my 45th Middlebury reunion, I stopped for coffee at Middlebury Market and ran into old colleague, Mike McKenna. I asked, "How ya doin?" and he responded with the old saw, "Well, still upright and grateful for that."

You get to a certain age and you're glad to be alive, merely.

That afternoon I saw my classmate, Margot Childs Cheel, whom I had actually dated a couple of times when we were in our 20s. She asked how I was, and I trotted out that day's expression.

"Still erect," I said cheerfully.

"Really," she said.

I realized my poor choice of words. "You know," I stammered, "upright, above ground, standing erect, alive."

"Right," she said.

Never too old to make a fool of myself.

Africa!

I'm just about the most provincial person I know. A trip to Burlington for me is a big deal. I have traveled much in Addison County. I am comforted by routine and familiarity.

So I'm a Yankee. Worse, I am a Swedish Yankee. I grew up in Maine and have lived in Vermont all this time. My dad's parents emigrated from Sweden. That side of the family is full of Nordic reserve.

Little do people know that beneath the placid surface we Yankees are a seething mass of anxiety. We like our comfort zones.

Yet . . . from August 2013 to June 2014, I lived in Yaounde, Cameroon, West Africa with my family: Brett, Annie (16), and Peter (18).

How did that come about? What was I doing in Africa?

Africa!

Africa was so far out of my comfort zone . . . it was out of my comfort *hemisphere*, out of my comfort *galaxy*.

Brett was up for a scheduled sabbatical and thought a Fulbright Fellowship would be a good idea. We should go away as a family, live somewhere else, before our kids were big and on their own. I agreed: good idea.

I couldn't sell Maine (we had spent another of her sabbatical years on the southern coast of Maine—idyllic), so I suggested British Columbia, Western Canada, 3000 miles away. A colleague had taken his family there for a sabbatical and had a good time.

"Canada? Really, Karl. Canada?"

"Okay, how about Ireland?" I had been to Ireland a couple times in my job at the College, visiting Irish universities. It was fascinating.

"No, not Ireland. Let's go somewhere and learn a different language," she said.

Sweden! I have never been there. My people!

Too cold.

Through a process of elimination, I figured we'd go to Spain. Warm. Culturally stimulating. Language immersion. Spain's okay, I thought, though a stretch for this Swedish Yankee. I can do that, I thought. Maybe.

Near the end of the summer, 2012, we were eating dinner on the back porch on a warm August night, when Brett told us she was applying for a Fulbright *in Africa*. "All things considered, that makes the most sense," she explained.

I was taken aback. Way back. I left the table and went for a little walk around the house. I composed myself and returned. I choked out, "What happened to Spain?"

Annie then checked in. Having just turned 15, she announced, "If I'm going to leave my friends at school and my sports teams, I want to go someplace really different. Spain is too cliché."

From then on, Africa for a year was a possibility. Then, in early spring, 2013, Brett was informed she had been awarded the Fellowship in Cameroon.

Yaounde Street Scene

Game on. I would be the "trailing spouse" of a Fulbright Fellow, an apt term.

When I told John Walsh, former Chaplain at Middlebury College, about our Africa plan at Reunions in June before leaving in August 2013, he beamed, clasped my arm and exulted, "This will be a life-changing experience!"

"John," I said, "that's what I'm afraid of."

First Day

Our first day in Cameroon, we took Peter and Annie to their school, the American School of Yaounde (ASOY), where the school year had already begun. Peter would be there for the fall and then start Middlebury in the spring, Annie for the full year.

We told the cab driver to take us to "l'ecole americaine."

After a one-hour drive through the teeming streets of Yaounde, the most harrowing ride any of us had ever taken, and the best possible introduction to our new home for the year, we arrived at the gate of the Rain Forest International School.

"No, no, monsieur," we told the driver, "l'*autre* ecole americaine!"

There are two American schools in Yaounde, the capital of Cameroon. RFIS is an evangelical Christian school, a boarding school, about 12–15 miles from centre ville.

Annoyed and frustrated, the driver made a few calls, and we retraced our route and landed at ASOY, only a short distance from where we started.

ASOY has a close relationship to the American Embassy, and a student body in 2013 of 148 students, K–12, from 40 different countries. About 20 percent of the students were American, the largest contingent the children of Americans teaching there. About 30 percent were Cameroonian; the rest from all over.

We met with Director Sheena Nabholz, a Pakistani-Canadian, recently arrived from Jordan to lead the school. After we settled

Peter and Annie, I mentioned to her that I had over 40 years of teaching experience: "If you ever need a substitute teacher in the high school, give me a call."

She did. That night. She asked me if I would teach two courses, AP English (with another teacher) and College Writing.

I said "Sure," and I'm so glad I did.

Creative Writing, Spring 2014:
Max, Brenda, Annie, Joyce, Jordi, Karl

I went to Cameroon with no particular plan. I would have led a lonely life had I not found a place at ASOY. Every morning during the week I climbed in the car with Peter and Annie (we hired Richard to be our driver—it would have taken me a long, long time to be comfortable driving in Yaounde) and we wound our way to ASOY where I would teach my classes and hang out in the Library. I enjoyed especially getting to know my expat American teaching colleagues for the year.

At home in our neighborhood in Yaounde, running water only ran about half the time, power outages were frequent, the internet quite undependable. It's hot in Cameroon, right on the Equator.

Brett's teaching of American literature was under very challenging circumstances at the overcrowded and under-resourced University of Yaounde. In the spring she had over 200 students and no books, only photocopies she made at her own expense.

ASOY, on the other hand, was air-conditioned, had a generator if the power failed, lots of bottled water, consistent internet reception. The kids I taught were lively and smart, classes were small (12 in AP English; six in College Writing in the fall, five in Creative Writing in the spring), the atmosphere generally positive and stimulating. I loved having the opportunity to teach my own kids.

My friend Rick couldn't believe they didn't pay me for teaching two courses at ASOY the whole year.

I couldn't believe they didn't *charge* me for teaching there!

Lindholm House

The admissions building at Bates College is the "Lindholm House," named after my dad. It's an elegant structure. I used to tell people I was such a star at Lewiston High that Bates named a building after me, but they generally didn't believe me.

I know the building at Middlebury I want to be named after me. At present, it is not named for anyone.

When I was a baseball player at Middlebury, a pitcher, the baseball field was behind the Sig Ep and Chi Psi fraternities on Porter Field Road, where the Mahaney Center for the Arts parking lot is now. It was a pretty long walk from the Field House where we changed into our uniforms to the playing field.

Baseball teams like to come out long before the actual start of the game to loosen up, take batting practice, and infield/outfield practice. The game finally starts a couple hours later.

Whenever I was scheduled to pitch, I was wracked by nerves, lots of adrenaline flowing—and that was not all that was flowing. I often had to take a leak at inopportune times.

It was hard to find a place to go when I had to go. To walk all the way back to the Field House took an unreasonable length of time. Usually, I just went clomp-clomping into one of the frat houses, and they were none too pleased with my baseball spikes on their wooden floors.

Once the game was held up for me while I was relieving myself. The Panthers went down one-two-three, and I came out from the basement of the Sig Ep house buttoning up as I hustled back to the mound.

Well, this embarrassing circumstance happens no longer, not since we built our new South Street baseball field in the 1990s.

It has a beautiful bathroom facility located between the baseball and softball fields. In the men's room (I haven't been in the women's room) there are two sinks, two stalls with toilets and two urinals. It's very spacious.

And here's the best part—it's heated! Sometimes, it's so cold at April baseball games that fans just go and huddle in the bathrooms to get warm.

So if the College wants to honor me for my innumerable contributions, it could do worse than name that facility at the baseball field the "Lindholm Lavatory."

I would be very proud.

Compensation

If you retire as an "emeritus" faculty member, a status I didn't deserve but was accorded, you are allowed to teach one course a year in retirement, so that's what I do.

It's great. I teach my class and don't go back to an office with a desk full of further responsibilities, some quite urgent, and an email inbox of notes impossible to respond to adequately, also quite urgent.

Instead, I go home and walk the dogs. Or I go to lunch with a friend.
Or I sit in my car in the parking lot behind Greg's Market eating my lunch, reading the *Boston Globe*, and listening to my daughter Jane's show "Vermont Edition" on VPR, perfectly content.

As I was trying to decide whether to take on a course, I ran into Chris Watters, retired from a long, distinguished career teaching biology at Middlebury. Every winter term, he teaches his killer cell biology course to pre-meds (who are decidedly not spending their January at the Snow Bowl and Two Brothers Tavern).

I asked him if he got paid for teaching this class.

"Nope. I don't get paid for teaching the course," he told me. "I get paid for grading the papers."

VGA HDMI

I wanted to show a YouTube video in my Winter Term class and was having trouble getting the sound to work on the system in my so-called "smart classroom."

This was something of an ongoing comedy routine. I amused students with my struggles with the technology that supports our teaching.

I appealed to the class for help. Tom, in the back, offered some friendly instruction: "Just unplug the 'aux cord'; it only works with the VGA. Then, plug in the HDMI . . ."

The blank look on my face caused him to get up and undertake himself what he suggested I do. Voila, sound with my video.

The older I get, the behinder I am.

Car Talk

My car is my refuge. I spend a lot of time in my car. I am proud of my car, a Prius with nearly 200,000 miles. I have a "beater" Prius, full of dents and bruises. It counters the liberal weenie stereotype.

I am ageless in my car, nothing in my body hurts. I am confident I can run again, play noon hoops, if I just do a little conditioning.

It's when I get out of my car that I am stiff and sore, wracked by mortality. I have ambition in the car; I make great plans that ultimately go unrealized.

For some men (me, for example), our car is the equivalent of a woman's pocketbook—a perfect mess. But it's our mess, perfect, and we like it that way.

I was headed to lunch with a former colleague. It was raining, so I suggested we drive downtown. My car was right there.

I noticed she hesitated to get in the passenger side. She was dressed nicely, professionally, as she was still working full time. I sensed she was put off by the condition of my car, the mess.

It may have been the newspapers and dog leash on the passenger's seat that I threw in the back, or the coffee and chocolate milk stains on the seat, now quite dry and harmless, or the general disarray (yes, even some trash in the back—food wrappers, plastic bottles and aluminum cans).

I pointed to the floor below her seat and said, "Oh, a mouse!"

She didn't find that amusing.
The next time we go to lunch (if in fact she agrees to have lunch again with me), we'll probably walk, or go in her (spotless) car.

Mortality

At our Class of 1967 reunions, we always have a session where we talk about our life stage. At our 45th, it was about retirement. Some of us were fully retired, others were partially retired, cutting back, and then some were still working full time. People would talk about why they made the choices they have.

I was mostly retired, though still teaching a class now and then.

The first two people who volunteered to talk went on and on about how great retirement was. One had become an environmental activist, adopted a whole new and exciting identity. Another waxed on and on about the joy of determining just how you want to spend your time that day.

Anne, my girlfriend in college (who wasn't there), worked in retirement advising other Baby Boomers how to productively spend their retirement years. She ran a consulting group called "Working Differently."

I listened as long as I could, and then asked the question that seemed to hang in the room, at least for me. "What about Death! How are you dealing with your mortality, the fact that pretty soon you're gonna die?

"Our parents have died, or are very old indeed; our beloved mentors are gone or are going fast; our friends and colleagues just a little older are passing away too. Public figures who were young when we were young are dying. We read obits and we never did before. We are surrounded by death."

We have reached the stage when, to quote Hemingway, "People are dying now who never died before."

At this stage, for me and my contemporaries, death is no longer an abstraction, or premature or accidental. We are confronted every day, in one way or another, with its immanence.

I'm not sure everyone appreciated my intrusion with that sentiment.

It's true that the challenge of retirement has to do with issues of identity and relevance, but the biggest challenge of all, and we don't often talk seriously about it, is accommodating the aging process and our own mortality.

We find ourselves wide awake at 3:00 in the morning, staring at the ceiling in a dark room, waiting, grateful to still be erect, that is, above ground, when dawn comes.

Papa Hemingway

I attended the banquet of the 50th reunion of the class of 1965, and enjoyed the communion with old friends. I had on my light summer sport coat. I thought I was looking sharp indeed.

My friend, Jeff McKay, insisted that in my advanced years, I had come to resemble Ernest Hemingway.

I demurred. "It's just the white beard and the girth," I said. "We really don't look that much alike."

He was insistent. He asked another old friend who was walking by, "What famous person do you think Karl looks like."

She looked me over for a minute and said, "Colonel Sanders!"

I no longer dare deny the resemblance to Papa Hemingway for fear of the alternative. Who's next—Grandpa Walton? Santa Claus?

No resemblance!

Hall of Fame

When I heard that a Middlebury Athletic Hall of Fame was contemplated as part of the new Field House project, I wrote to the Big Dogs suggesting that it was a bad idea.

We didn't need one, I argued. It would just cause hard feelings when one athlete got in and another didn't—or this sport had too many, or the gender balance was off.

I worried that development concerns might intrude—i.e. this alum played a sport and is poised to make a big gift to the College; or emotions would be engaged—i.e. it would mean a lot to a beloved but not-altogether-successful coach; or...well you can imagine the myriad subjective possibilities.

I discovered this position had allies in the Athletic Department itself. After all, we promote the idea that sports are about participation, teamwork, not individual glory.

In the end, there was little debate. We would have an Athletic Hall of Fame.

So I quickly pivoted from principle to pragmatism, expressing my interest and willingness to be a part of the process of selecting who should be included this exalted group.

At my age, hypocrisies of this sort are not uncommon.

We've picked our fourth Hall of Fame class now, and it's been a most enjoyable part of my retirement life at Middlebury. I am a member of a 10-person committee that examines candidates and recommends from five to ten athletes each year to be honored.

With a century-old history of athletics at Middlebury (and nearly a half-century of brilliant women's teams), every person selected is eminently qualified. The induction ceremony in November is a very good time indeed.

The by-laws require that we have at least one inductee from the pre-NESCAC (1973) era. I enjoy doing the archival research into that group, my contemporaries, and those notables, some long forgotten, who went before.

When asked about my role on the committee, I say, "I research the dead guys, because that's the group closest to me in age."

Competence

In retirement, you stop doing the things you're best at, the things you spent literally a lifetime working on.

I don't claim I was better than others in my position at Middlebury, the Deans. But I knew what I was doing. I knew the institution. When a student came in with a problem or an idea, I knew what was possible.

I knew the ins and outs of the system. In the Middlebury system, the Deans had considerable authority in the day-to-day lives of students. More so than at other places. We could tell them yes, or no. They might be disappointed with our response, but they weren't given the runaround. On a daily basis, I felt competent to deal with student issues and crises.

My best days were when I solved a problem for a student, or collaborated with a faculty colleague on thorny problem, or spoke to an anxious parent, and I knew that these parties left with a confidence that they were dealing with someone who knew what he was doing, a professional.

In retirement, this lifetime of training is largely for naught. You have time to do the myriad practical tasks that were so hard to schedule before—getting the snow tires put on the car or cars (not to mention inspections), getting a haircut, making sure there's milk in the fridge, and so on.

You do have more time to read and write and answer properly those emails from friends that went unanswered before. You have time to read an actual newspaper, a delight, if anachronistic, in these days of e-communication.

Still it's hard to escape the feeling that the things you were best at, you can no longer do, and that sense of loss is detrimental to self-regard.

So sometimes you ask yourself, what am I good at now?

Men of '67

My three best friends, friends since college, live right here with me in Middlebury or nearby: Gary Margolis, my roommate sophomore and junior years and colleague for all my years at Middlebury; Peter Lebenbaum, a child psychologist who moved to Middlebury in 1983; and Rick Hawley, a brilliant and prolific writer in many forms, who retired to Ripton after being headmaster at University School for 20 years.

Gary, Rick, Karl, and Peter: Awesome Foursome

We spend a lot of time with one another.

My other best friend from college, Jon Coffin, lived in Burlington for most of my 40 years in Middlebury, just up the road. He now lives in Brunswick, Maine, just a few hundred yards from my sister, Martha, whom I often visit.

How lucky am I?

Cute

Last entry.

I have just finished a long September weekend at Bread Loaf, Middlebury's mountain campus, with 30 of my 1967 classmates, planning our upcoming 50th college reunion.

50 years! Seems like a good place to stop.

I have attended all of my Middlebury reunions, except for the first in 1972 when work obligations, teaching school, precluded taking the time off. I live here in Middlebury—it was convenient for me to attend and I always had a good time, getting to know classmates who were not my friends in college.

I remember at these reunions every five years observing and celebrating the members of the 50th class, the oldest among us as a group, leading the parade of classes up the hill from Old Chapel to Convocation in Mead Chapel.

We applauded these grandpas and grandmas—hoary of pate, wrinkled of visage, lumpy in form.

We nodded to one another, comfortable in our resilient youth, and thought, "Aren't they cute."

Now they're us!

Goodness.

Acknowledgements

Many thanks to Barbara Bentley, whose early and ongoing support was crucial; Lyn DeGraff of Alumni and Parent Programs for her design skills and enthusiasm for the project; and classmates Peter Kovner, Susan Patterson, Roxanne Leighton, and Don Elliman for their interest and support. I am also grateful to Blair Kloman for her expertise and encouragement. Heartfelt thanks, friends.

Introduction by

David Stameshkin
Middlebury College Historian

David Stameshkin, a 1967 graduate of the University of Chicago, earned his Ph.D. in history at the University of Michigan and taught at Middlebury College briefly in the 1970s, before spending 34 years as an administrator and history professor at Franklin & Marshall College in Lancaster, PA. Stameshkin has written three books on the history of Middlebury College, as well as a comic memoir, *The F**ket List: Things I Will NOT Be Doing Before I Die*. David and his wife, Colleen, a philosophy professor, are both retired. They live in Lancaster during much of the year, but spend their summers in a little cabin on beautiful Lake Dunmore, just south of Middlebury.

CPSIA information can be obtained
at www.ICGtesting.com
Printed in the USA
FFHW011343010519
52157267-57526FF